WILDFOWL
MAGAZINE'S
DUCK
HUNTING

WILDFOWL
MAGAZINE'S
DUCK
HUNTING

Best of *Wildfowl*'s Skills, Tactics, and Techniques from Top Experts

INTRODUCTION BY
SKIP KNOWLES

Skyhorse Publishing

Skyhorse Publishing books may be purchased in bulk at special discounts for sales promotion, corporate gifts, fund-raising, or educational purposes. Special editions can also be created to specifications. For details, contact the Special Sales Department, Skyhorse Publishing, 307 West 36th Street, 11th Floor, New York, NY 10018 or info@skyhorsepublishing.com.

Skyhorse® and Skyhorse Publishing® are registered trademarks of Skyhorse Publishing, Inc.®, a Delaware corporation.

Visit our website at www.skyhorsepublishing.com.

10 9 8 7 6 5 4 3

Library of Congress Cataloging-in-Publication Data is available on file.

Cover design by Stephan Ledeboer and Tom Lau
Cover photo by Dale C. Spartas, www.spartasphoto.com. The hunt was provided by Northern Prairie Outfitters, www.northenprairieoutfitters.com

Print ISBN: 978-1-5107-1910-1
Ebook ISBN: 978-1-5107-1911-8

Printed in China

TABLE OF CONTENTS

INTRODUCTION

IN THE BLOOD

Duck hunters don't have to wait to go to heaven. For us it exists right here, all fall and winter. So why do people think we're crazy? A friend who hunts upland birds once asked me why duck hunters are willing to endure all they suffer through. Struggling in mud that will suck your boots off or breaking ice just to get soaked throwing decoys in the dark. "How is that fun?" he asked. The 4 a.m. starts over freezing boat ramps or in sleet and rain, building brushy blinds all summer in the heat and insects, and the stinky wet dogs shaking water and mud and blood on everything . . . all while hauling grimy, expensive and always-breaking paraphernalia. Living with the mountains of expensive decoys, overpriced ATVs and specialized boats good for just one place: The swamps that most people avoid at all cost.

It is all rather unappealing to a refined tweedy upland birder with a glossy double gun and a pretty fair-weather dog with frills hanging off its tail.

There is so much I want to tell him. How those mission-specific boats and gear are ugly aesthetically, yes, but very beautiful to us. How a handmade heated floating portable dog blind you killed a weekend building (hey, the thing almost works) totally made sense at the time you were trying to re-purpose that old Igloo cooler.

Because you're holding this book, you get it, but how do you explain?

That to you, waterfowling is so rich in diversity, pageantry and lore, no other avenue in the hunting life is as noble. That nothing stirs you like the skinny fingers of daybreak reaching out in quicksilver traces through your decoys as dawn peeps across a marsh.

We can give ourselves goose bumps at any time just by closing our eyes and thinking of ducks and geese on their final approach to the layout blind, as you hold your breath and try to become small and invisible.

How we love all that filthy gear, that post-apocalyptic boat/blind, that messy pile of decoys in need of paint, those ragged bags full of fake birds, that wobbly old MOJO with the steel shot pellets embedded beak to butt. That dirty layout blind in the corner of the garage. These are our weapons, our tools of the trade, not encumbrances. Magic things happen when we climb in a blind and look to the sky.

There is simply nothing like waterfowling. How the hiss of wings cutting the air before you have even seen the birds can be louder than you can believe, as your stomach knots up at the realization *they are really close.* How often before you have seen them you catch that flicker of motion reflected across the surface of the water, the speeding shadows of these much-awaited sky-born creatures that fly as fast as arrows.

With time, you know their language and can tell by their chatter whether they are happy or nervous birds even on the approach. And just by the shifting sounds their wings make you can tell if they have seen you or not. How do you explain that when you are washed in the blood it is not so much work, as it must appear to a genteel quail hunter, but truly living?

Heaven to you is friends and family in a blind, the 10 a.m. smell of propane and cooking sausage creeping through the cold dense air, inside a boat or a hide where even little people's legs are long enough to join in the fun. Your subconscious registers the *thump-thump-thump* of a Lab's tail telling you to hurry and scan the skies for approaching silhouettes. "Everybody get down, here they come!"

Hunting is a reminder that not all men can be tamed, and waterfowlers are the Wild Bunch of bird hunting. Each fall, everyone who is not crazy is home watching football, sleeping in, eating Christmas turkey . . . where is the reward in that? How intensely alive and happily weary do you feel coming home after a day of snow and boat spray and wind in your face? It's a much different kind of tired, a pleasant warm glow, many worlds removed from the fatiguing stress of career and day-to-day modern life.

But I don't tell all this to my pheasant-chasing friend. Instead, I put it in terms I knew he could grasp: Imagine if the pheasants or Huns or quail came in 15 different subspecies, every brilliant color under the sun? Now imagine if giant flocks of pheasants showed up overnight and covered entire fields when just weeks prior there were none in your area. A few show up, and they start migrating through by the tens of thousands? What if you eagerly watched for storms to the far north to bring the harbinger, the forefront of this migration? Now imagine you could call those upland birds in and decoy them in huge flocks and shoot them right in front of a comfortable blind with friends.

That's why we do it.

I love upland bird hunting. There is something great about just grabbing a gun and going for a walk. It is a simple pleasant experience, like golf, an enhanced stroll in the outdoors, and the explosion of a pheasant's flush is thrilling. But neither pheasants nor Chukar nor Huns are even native wildlife (though they are delicious). And the dog work is not remotely the same. Training a Lab to launch off your boat or blind and land with a heavy splash, already lined out and chasing a drake pintail, breaking skim ice, even diving for a cripple, it is as intense as gun dog-work gets.

And the wingshooting is far more challenging. Calling a flock of greenheads shining in the sun in close, seeing them buckle their wings in commitment, and folding a duck clean to splash in the water is as close to a major league home run as us amateur athletes are going to get. Standing up in a rolling boat and killing a drake sea duck that is screaming like a fighter jet with a tail wind, or successfully shooting a single bird from a clump of dainty teal doing their drunken flock-of-bats flight approach . . . you do that, and you know you have done something.

WILDFOWL has been there . . . over 30 years and going strong, surprising, no doubt, to those who thought print content—both books and magazines—would go the way of VHF and compact discs. While internet content has improved slightly, it's not happening nearly fast enough. "Blue-facing" your way through websites to try and find meaningful, immersive features and stories is still an unpleasant experience wherein unwanted auto insurance pop-up ads and videos are blaring at you, as you navigate a sea of intrusive prompts, many of which are phony attempts to get you to click-through to an unrelated advertiser's site. It is all rather annoying, and you can't even see your device's screen well in bright light or sunshine. We live in fear of getting wet and if your tablet or phone's battery doesn't die, you still have to shut it down when planes take off.

That will change, surely, but for now what decent web content exists mostly remains lost in a sprawling wasteland wherein guys who have never called a bird are trying to tell you how to do it. Readers know every time they grab an issue of *WILDFOWL* they are going to learn something, be treated to exciting new gear and go on a few great hunts within those pages. This book provides a hell of a lot of those pages as it is comprised entirely of features from the magazine. Between these covers, we have illustrated the glorious diversity that waterfowling offers, with clear, honest writers who bring you along for their misses as much as their hits. There are just so many ways and species, times and places, in which to duck hunt, it is outrageous. From king eiders and magnificent long-tailed ducks out on the salt, to the cathedral of silence when standing amid timber in a blackwater swamp, to sunny cut-corn greenhead shoots, it would be very difficult to experience everything waterfowling has to offer in just one lifetime. The open ocean, the wind-blown points on lakes, tiny ponds, ditches, breakwaters, flooded fields, dry fields, deep swamps of flooded timber; all these become your playground.

If you need solace and solitude, you will find it out in a marsh. Inversely, it can be the most social of all hunting. If you wish to spend quality time with a youth and drive home a work ethic in a positive fun environment, take the family. Fair-weather waterfowling can be some of the very best times to spend with children. I love big game hunting, and it certainly brought its own milestones growing up, but my best childhood memories are not of sitting in a deer stand freezing, waiting and willing for something, anything, to happen. Those memories are more of frozen toes and watching squirrels. It can be a rush, but you can go years without so much as firing a shot on that side of the hunting experience.

No, my best memories are of chasing my father, bushwhacking our way through south Texas coastal salt marsh, a limit of ducks bobbing over his shoulder. The beauty and variety of those birds, the excitement, the action and smoking shotgun shells plopping in the mud, these are vivid. Stopping to wet a line or try to catch a potful of big blue crabs redfish or fresh oysters. A kid with a .410 trying to act like a man, killing coots by age five. Adventure waited just around every bend in those little briny rivers. We zipped through narrow winding creeks, once hitting an errant alligator. The breathtaking thrill of laying on my back watching the geese come back to roost in the evening with my father laying silent beside me, the birds making so much noise it was nearly over-stimulation for a youngster, and the mesmerizing movement of waves upon waves of graceful birds crossing the sky above us.

How could you ever stop wanting to experience that? A true waterman in the Chesapeake mold, where we were both born, Dad would shoot a cottonmouth with his old Fox double, reload and kill a passing pintail without a flinch. Many wild boars and the occasional big buck fell to that old gun while running around that marsh too. He killed three hogs one night out there. He gave one of the pigs to two guys back at the boat ramp once they agreed to help him load his car-topper skiff and the other two pigs in the back of his old blue two-wheel drive GMC pickup, sliding them over the wooden floorboards of the bed.

We jump-shot birds a lot back then, but even as opportunistic jump shooters, Dad employed a cunning strategy. We'd flush the birds in one spot, then get set up on it with a few decoys, while someone else took off to jump shoot a few other spots so the buzzing ducks would circle and land on us. Simple, fast-paced, and so much fun. Dad once fell face-down in a muddy trail and found himself nose-to-nose with a big deadly cottonmouth. His best friend Ned Chesire took out what was left of Pa's hearing with a muzzle blast right over his head, vaporizing the serpent.

From the Columbia Basin of Eastern Washington to Florida, Texas, and other places we lived, he created a hunting vagabond in me, instilling both a self-respect found in outdoor challenges and a deep respect for the wilds. Back then, we never even thought to chase the majestic Harlequin ducks and black brant close to our Seattle home, species I would later come to covet as spectacular trophy birds. The running joke in my company is that I have another family in Argentina, where duck flights are so non-stop you never have enough ammo on hand, and Mexico's waterfowling has proven a favorite, with bonus dove-shooting each evening in the mildest winter weather imaginable.

It's a grand way to see the world, as a hunter, for your venture to places other travelers will never go. Regardless of whether you ever roam abroad chasing feathers, you may do so in these pages. Some of us were lucky to be born into it, but these days many of us who are joining the sport were not. Whether it's pop culture influence (*Duck Dynasty*), hipsters yearning to connect with the wild, or just wanting to eat healthy organic meat, or the explosion in female hunters and intelligent youth-recruitment programs, there are many of us with a yearning to learn and have some guidance into the sport. The best way to learn is not to force yourself to read tactics or boring advice from how-to manuals, but rather to take intimate tours on adventures through the eyes of those who have been there. This book gives you that opportunity, while entertaining with humor and immersive tales by hunters who have learned much from doing things both wrong and right. Reading these stories, you will learn what you need to know: How to dope the wind, how many decoys to use and where to put them; where the best opportunities lay, even how to create your own duck hunting property. And you will do it while being led on adventures all over this great continent and a few others, expeditions that veteran waterfowlers will also enjoy escaping into.

With access more complicated these days, modern waterfowling takes a little more planning and logistics than bygone eras. Like Dad and I discovered when we went back to that salt marsh almost 20 years later . . . it had changed but we still found lots of birds. We just had to work harder while coming to terms with the fact that many other people had now invaded "our" place. Helping you know what to do is a large part of what this book is for.

That Texas marsh will always be just that, though . . . our place. Acquiring your own expertise and rich nostalgic traditions will happen through your experiences afield, but studying your craft and the lore of waterfowling need not be a burden. It should be fun. Immerse yourself in this book, get fired up while learning along the way, and go make your own rich memories.

This book may not make you a total expert on waterfowling, but you will learn a hell of a lot, and venture many new exciting places as well. —*Skip Knowles, Editor, WILDFOWL Magazine*

SECTION ONE
TACTICS

PRIME TIME
for Ducks

Hunt the early season as hard as you
do the late, and you have the advantage.

BY JOE ARTERBURN

© Joe Genzel

YOU KNOW THOSE EARLY-SEASON ducks, the ones that pile into your decoys on opening day like they've never seen a decoy, because most are not old enough to have ever seen one? The yearlings, the ones with no inkling you're waiting in a freshly-camouflaged blind or hunkered in the tules with a quivering Lab by your side?

It doesn't take a duck-hunting genius to have a bang-up opener on those ducks, but the real question is not only how do you kill ducks when the migration is just getting started, but also how do you stretch your success well into the season—and be in the zone, ready to rock when the migrators start pouring in? There's plenty you can do to assure consistent success during early-season and beyond.

It's a dang good bet your success rate will drop off after opening weekend if you take those local ducks for granted. The key, according to Banded's Chad Belding, is to not get lazy, but apply real effort in hunting those early-season ducks, with as much attention to detail as when you hunt the wizened, call-shy flocks as they wing south through a gauntlet of hunters.

Belding lives in Nevada but as host of "The Fowl Life," he hunts all over North America. Mark Schafer, on the other hand, concentrates on small waters near the North Platte River in Nebraska. Both are dedicated hunters who start watching the skies as summer wanes. Early on they start thinking about sprucing up decoys and getting out the camo shotgun. Repairs or improvements to blinds, heck, that's already done.

"Early season is just a riot," Schafer said. "They pile in the decoys like

you owe them money. Around here, it's oddball ducks, everything and anything might come in…wigeon, gadwall, blue-winged teal, green-winged teal, the occasional mallard. In the early season, it's tougher to pick out mallard drakes, which aren't in full plumage yet. And, there's something to learn from that, according to Belding. Since there is not a lot of color on ducks that time of year, there should not be

a lot of color in your decoy spread. Use decoys with less-flashy browns, blacks and earth tones, he said.

Once shotguns start blasting, it doesn't take long for ducks to figure out where they don't want to be and to start looking for somewhere they won't get hammered every time they put out their feet to land.

And that leads to Belding's next tip: "Scouting is underestimated during the early season. Find where

© Joe Genzel

ducks are going to seek respite from the early-season gunfire, maybe a waterfowl refuge and, more importantly, where they are going to feed and loaf when they leave the refuge.

"You need to find where those ducks are hitting after that initial onslaught they face opening weekend," Belding said.

THE RIG

Then, it's a matter of setting up. Schafer sets his decoys with a big open area in the middle, with one sacrificial marker decoy set at 40 yards, using a laser rangefinder to get it exact, and "everything inside that decoy is fair game," he said. That, he said, is especially useful in helping young hunters know when and where to shoot when he calls the shot.

Motion is important, Schafer said. He uses Wonderducks, usually three or four, with spinning legs that propel them on the water, creating movement and ripples. "And, we might use a Wonderduck with spinning wings that doesn't splash, but we usually don't use the spinning-wing decoys on the pole until the mallards get here," he said.

Belding suggests a Mojo spinning-wing decoy, but not in the middle of the set. Try something unexpected, like placing it in the reeds on the perimeter so overhead ducks catch just a glimpse of movement.

"We use a single pull cord early season with three decoys set out in the middle of the opening in the decoys," Schafer said.

Also, you don't need a lot of decoys, Belding said, because local ducks aren't used to seeing huge concentrations of ducks and won't see them until migrators start coming in. A couple dozen is plenty.

Nor should you overdo calling in the early season, Schafer said. Some mild quacking is OK, and whistles are good. You don't have to do much calling, just get their attention.

"It's the perfect time to shoot your favorite 20-gauge at close-decoying smaller ducks," Schafer said. "Or, if you're dead set on using your 12-gauge, take 2¾-inch 3s or 4s."

MUDDY WATERS
In addition to motion in the decoys, both Schafer and Belding are proponents of muddying the water in and around the decoy set.

so a view from ducks flying overheard of decoys floating on crystal

"Early season is just a riot. They pile in the decoys like you owe them money."

Ducks landing, swimming and feeding naturally stir the water, clear water does not look natural. Periodically wading through the

decoys and sending your dog through helps produce the desired effect. Before the hunt even starts, Schafer throws a bumper a few times so his Lab, Abby, stirs the water while burning off nervous energy.

"A lot of people think it's going to be an easy deal and ducks are going to see our fake decoys and they're going to come flying in and just want to die," Belding said. "We owe it to the birds and ourselves to get them as close as possible no matter the time of year and get clean, ethical shots."

Belding refers to it as getting ducks into the "arc of vulnerability."

"As a duck hunter, we have to make sure we create a notion of submissiveness in ducks flying in to create vulnerability in those ducks," he said. "Ducks already

have the upper hand on hunters with their birds-eye view. And they've been seeing live ducks their whole life. It may be early-season, but they still have a memory, they know what real ducks look like, they know what they saw last season or the younger ducks have been seeing throughout the summer. Why give them even the slightest opportunity to pick you apart after you've instilled a little vulnerability in them? They're coming your way, they've heard your call, everything looks real and sounds real; now stay hidden without bright skin shining or dogs moving. Let them see the movement in the decoys, the ripples, the chocolate-milk effect of the muddy water."

Now you're not doing things like an average duck hunter. You're

thinking like a duck and thinking if you're that duck in the air what is going to make you vulnerable.

"You want them to become so comfortable with you that they trust you," "Those ducks trust you are the real thing because you have taken the time to do all the little things that make it look real."

FIRST HUNT DUCKS

With the excitement of opening morning, it's smart to set or reinforce ground rules, especially if you have new hunters in the blind, said Schafer, who often invites youngsters along, introducing them to duck hunting.

"When in the blind for the first time of the season, I run through the rules, even stuff like gun safety and wearing ear plugs," he said.

The big jar of ear plugs in the blind emphasizes his point.

"So everyone knows where to look, I tell them the front of the blind is 12 o'clock, the right is 3 o'clock, the left is 9 o'clock and I'm going to tell you where on the clock the ducks are coming from and give you ample warning and when I tell you to shoot, if you are on the right side shoot the closest duck on the right side; if you're in the middle, shoot the closest duck in the middle," he said. "Usually with novice duck hunters, everybody shoots the lowest duck on the right, so you have one duck blown to heck and the rest of the ducks flying away laughing. Everyone needs to shoot their lane."

Schafer tells them to pick one duck and keep shooting at it until they are certain it's going down. "A rookie mistake is to take one shot at this duck, one shot at that duck and one shot at another and end up with nothing," he said.

"I also don't let anyone hold their gun or even pick it up until I tell them to," he said. "Ducks rarely sneak up on us and they are never armed. In 22 seasons, we've never had an accident."

And let guys know they can't swat cripples until given permission because the dog will be going.

Finally, Schafer said, "We always start the day with a word of prayer. You pray over your food, don't you? We give thanks we live in a country where we can do this and we pray for safety."

Decoy Dilemmas

Stop skittish flights from skirting the edges, learn when to hit "reset," and put the birds where they belong—in shotgun range

BY MARK ROMANACK

WITH SKILLFULLY-CRAFTED body shapes, unbelievable feather detail, flocked surfaces that mimic real birds and built-in motion, why, with the aid of these life-like decoys, do we still find ducks and geese thumbing their noses at our spreads?

High quality decoys certainly help hunters harvest more birds, but ducks and geese have an amazing ability to tell the difference between real birds and fakes. Accepting the fact many decoys are often just that to the eyes of waterfowl is the first step in getting the most from your days afield. Any hunter who has set up near live fowl knows the frustration of watching flocks approach only to peel off at the last second and land among the real birds. This happens so commonly that seasoned hunters often try to scare away birds on the ground.

Amazingly, when conditions are right, the most Spartan of rigs will lure in birds like moths to the flame. When hunts turn cold, it seems only the juvies, who haven't felt the concussion of shotgun fire, are foolish enough to stray within range.

The way to get the most from any decoy set is understanding its limitations, why they are sometimes a deal-breaker and how to use them as effectively as possible. Legions of duck hunters have grown up with rather rigid guidelines on how to best use decoys. Our fathers taught us stuff like rigging blocks so they all face into the wind and the theory that bigger decoy spreads outdraw smaller ones. I vividly remember when "super-magnum" decoys were believed to always be better than life-sized blocks.

There are some truths in these old standards, but they're not absolutes. Every situation is unique, because birds are going to have varying degrees of "survival experience." Lightly-pressured fowl can easily be duped with conventional wisdom. Refuge birds that fly the gauntlet and dance with the devil every day become so shy it's almost impossible to kill one on purpose.

To lure pressured migrators you need an edge, and that involves defying conventions once thought sacred.

SIZING UP THE SPREAD

Setting 150-plus decoys doesn't always make the spread more appealing. On calm days, there's less motion, so more decoys means you have more stagnant fakes, and the birds may avoid your rig for a smaller one. The average flock sizes working a particular area also factor into determining the best spread size. If most of the birds approaching a decoy rig show up in small groups, stick with smaller numbers.

On the other hand, if you're targeting large flocks of mallards, divers or Canada geese and facing competition from other hunters in the same area, a bigger spread can have the impact of focusing the bird's attention where you want it.

Mud will take the shine off layouts, and works on new decoys too. Just be sure to rinse off the fakes before setting up.

Fifteen years ago, I would set out four-dozen mallard floaters and a half-dozen geese over a small Saskatchewan pothole. But hunting pressure has become very light, and I've gradually decreased the amount of blocks I deploy. Today, I'm much more comfortable using only 12 duck floaters and two or three bonus geese. For field shoots in Saskatchewan I used to set out a total of 12-dozen various mallard and Canada goose decoys, but reduced it to two-dozen full-body geese and 18 mallard full-bodies.

Where you set your decoys is way more important than how many you use. We seldom have the luxury of always having access to hunt the exact spot the birds are favoring. Back home in Michigan, I'm more likely trying to pull birds to a single field or pothole. If you can be on the "X," a smaller decoy spread (in most instances) is going to be superior. But, if you're forced to lure birds outside their normal flight path, bigger is usually better.

SILHOUETTE REFLECTION

Decoys run the gamut from flocked full-bodies to silhouettes, spinners, windsocks, and rags...and they all have a time and place. I used to set a lot of silhouettes mixed in with shells and full-bodies, adding more fakes at a lower cost. One day I was struggling to get birds to commit to a spot I knew they really wanted.

Flock after flock would lock in, and as they naturally flanked the decoys to finish into the wind, the birds would peel off, make another pass and eventually disappear.

Luckily, a lone goose came over the spread and I crippled it. The bird sailed about 200 yards and crashed to the ground. I sent my Lab on the retrieve and followed him so I could cast the dog to the exact location the bird fell. When I turned back towards the decoys I could see exactly why we were getting busted. It was sunny and windy that particular day, and the silhouettes were wobbling back-and-forth, sending out flashes of light as if a dozen people were sitting in the corn stubble with signaling mirrors! I laid every silhouette flat on the ground and from that point on the flocks decoyed like we had them under remote control.

Now I take a little time to back away and survey the situation before each hunt, looking for potential problems. It's also led me to be suspicious of decoys for other reasons. Have you ever noticed how new blocks don't seem to work as well as the old and worn ones? I believe this is because freshly-painted decoys have more sheen on the surface than those long worn by sun and use.

It's true manufacturers paint their products with flat paints designed to keep glare to a minimum. Still, I feel a new or recently painted decoy is more likely to make birds nervous than older blocks.

SEEING THE LIGHT

Flocking closely mimics the natural iridescent color shades and hues found on popular waterfowl species. Also, because the surface of flocked decoys are porous compared to ordinary painted versions, light tends to absorb into the surface of the decoy rather than reflecting off.

How light reflects off a decoy or other gear used in duck hunting has fascinated me for years. My study of light reflection as it relates to duck hunting actually started because I noticed photographs I was taking seemed to illuminate some items in the image differently than others.

For example, I noticed when I photographed a hunter wearing the typical hard-surfaced nylon hunting coat, light reflected off the jacket almost like you would expect light to reflect off a smooth hard surface. A little experimentation and I soon learned certain fabrics absorb light and blend into the natural background while others reflect it and stand out. Wool and fleece absorb light because the fabric is porous, while smooth-surfaced polyester and nylon tend to reflect light because these fabrics are more tightly woven.

These days, I blend in better by wearing camouflaged wool and fleece garments that do an excellent job of absorbing light instead of reflecting it. If the new decoys you just bought are flocked, chances are they will work as well as the old and worn ones you're replacing. A simple fix for decoys that are not flocked is to dull up the paint finishes a little using a soft brush and some old fashioned marsh mud—just like mudding up a layout blind—and then rinse the decoys off.

Anyone who has hunted over decoys probably has noticed in

low light conditions birds tend to work the spread and finish properly. But, the brighter it gets the more cautious birds become, and may land outside the decoy spread or flare off altogether.

This occurs because in strong light the birds have the advantage of more closely scrutinizing the decoy rig. Ambient lighting plays a major role in how approaching waterfowl see a decoy spread. In sunny conditions with the light behind the birds, a decoy spread is going to look just like a bunch of plastic fakes. On the same sunny day, if the birds have to approach the decoys with the sun in their faces, the decoys will silhouette and it becomes much harder for birds to spot the same blocks as fakes.

Refuge birds that fly the **gauntlet** and **dance with the devil** every day become so shy it's almost impossible to kill one on purpose.

STOP FLOCK WATCHING

The art of decoy hunting is a slippery slope because the lessons we think we're learning one day, don't necessarily apply or pay off the next. The variables involved in hunting waterfowl over decoys are too numerous to pin down, let alone control. Some fundamental concepts can help us as hunters better understand what's going on when birds that look committed suddenly flare.

Most importantly as hunters we need to recognize problems quickly and try to fix them rather than stubbornly accepting fail-

ure. The next time you're hunting ducks or geese over decoys consider letting the first flock or two work in without shooting the second they're in range. If you watch the birds closely on their final approach they will give you clues about what isn't right. Often just moving the decoys or layout a little makes a huge difference in how approaching birds work.

When the birds aren't finishing, it's best to make changes immediately. The reality of hunting over decoys is for every bird that plops down in the pocket, there are going to be many others that resist that temptation.

Last year on a field hunt, we got my truck stuck in the mud and spent the whole morning digging out. We didn't even set our first decoy until about 10 a.m.

In our haste to get set up, we threw together a decoy spread and hid our layout blinds along the edge of some sparse cattails. Approaching birds soon started skirting our rig and landing just outside of shotgun range, adding to an already frustrating morning. After missing out on most of the early flights, I was reluctant to waste more precious hunting time resetting the decoys.

After about three more potential shooting opportunities ended in

birds passing us by, I could take it no more. We all pitched in and opted to move our layout blinds and toss several decoys further upwind creating a much bigger landing pocket. Within a few minutes, we were back in our blinds and had birds rocketing into the pocket.

As hunters, we hate to waste a minute of our precious hunting time. But sometimes resetting the decoys makes a huge difference in how birds respond to the spread. Sitting tight and hoping for the best is rarely the right decision.

Bills
PAST DUE

Give the hardy scaup a shot and you'll probably fall in love with this foul-weather bird.

BY KEN BAILEY

Heavy, dark clouds scudded across the gun-metal grey sky, racing to stay ahead of the west wind. I squinted against the rain and spray, my hand hard on the throttle, eyes glued to the fast approaching island. You won't find Nettle Island on any map; I call it that simply because it's an apt description of the three-acre bump rising from the sandy bottom of my favorite waterfowling lake. To the untrained eye it holds little attraction, its hummocky surface supporting only a forest of chin-high stinging nettle and a couple dozen willow skeletons stripped of all signs of life by the generations of cormorants who've made the island their nesting ground.

Swinging the jon boat into the wind, I eased it against Nettle Island's cobbled shore, hopped out and tied off. It looked to be the perfect day—an October chill in the air, low clouds and a steady wind. I smiled assuredly, as just off the east side of Nettle Island lays the largest bed of sago pondweed on the 40-square mile lake. In October, sago beds mean ducks, diving ducks,

Once you experience the bluebill's hell-bent manner of swinging on your blocks, you'll never forget it.

and especially bluebills. These are the days and the ducks I live for.

I'm not sure when my passion for hunting bluebills was born. More properly called scaup, bluebills—or just "bills" to the waterfowling fraternity—are mid-sized, rather non-descript birds, though the drakes do sport a handsome plumage of black and white, offset by fiercely yellow eyes. As with many of the diving ducks, however, they're thought of as "mud" ducks by many hunters, meaning poor table fare, though I would suggest this opinion is typically proffered only by those who've never eaten one.

The first bluebill I ever shot was as a teenager, hunting over a mid-sized wetland in western Manitoba's Minnedosa pothole country. It was only the second duck I'd ever downed and, thinking back, I probably could not have identified it as a bluebill if my life had depended on it. All I cared was that I'd just shot a duck, a pretty rare and special occasion at the time. Over the years,

as my passion for waterfowling grew, so too did my fervor for hunting diving ducks. Twenty-minute, full-limit grain field mallard shoots quickly lost their appeal and, as the years passed, I found myself hunting the big water and, more specifically, bluebills, whenever I could get away. I came to love the tradition, the boats, the blinds, the big staging wetlands, the weather, the wet retrievers, the extensive decoy rigs and hunts measured in hours rather than minutes.

Bluebills are a happy-go-lucky duck, firm, plump and game to the core, with a nervous, restless nature that keeps them flying in virtually all weather. Even on the sunniest, warmest fall days—those dreaded bluebirds—I can count on a few bills near preferred feeding sites. What they really seem to love, however, is harsh weather, "duck weather," and they'll stick it out long after the redheads and canvasbacks have departed for more temperate climes. As an ardent

wingshooter, few targets bring out my enthusiasm like a bill.

BLIND TRUST

Bills are hunter-friendly in that they don't seem to care how well your blind is constructed. Provided you keep your face down and don't move when they're on final approach, they'll generally commit. On Nettle Island, in fact, I seldom set up a blind, electing to sit along the shoreline, where the dense vegetation behind me eliminates any chance that my silhouette will give me away. On big marshes, camouflage clothing and the discipline to not peek is generally all it takes.

Once you experience the bluebill's hell-bent manner of swinging on your blocks, you'll never forget it. Permanently etched in my mental scrapbook, for example, is the image of squadron after squadron of bills screaming through our decoys as a friend and I sat perched on the craggy shore of a small granite island on Great Slave Lake's north

GOOD EATIN'

arm. They came in groups of sixes, 10s, 20s and 30s, flight after flight, assaulting our blocks like F-18s on a strafing run, their wings folded back as they steered with their tails. As bills are wont to do they came in low, twisting on the wind, before climbing back out in sharp, high-G turns. We spent two days hunting from that island and long before we'd collected our 25-bird limit we put our shotguns down, settled back among the rocks and watched the amazing aerial show repeat itself again and again against the wilderness backdrop of the remote boreal landscape.

FAVORED SPREADS

Bluebills are a gregarious bird by nature. They love the company of other ducks and can often be found in large rafts, often mixed with canvasbacks or redheads. On a recent hunt on Lake of the Woods, on the Minnesota-Ontario border, we searched in vain for the better part of a day for the bills we knew should be there. When we finally found them they were in rafts numbering several hundred birds each, idling the day away as they rode the foam-flecked waves. The bluebill's proclivity for company usually means that the bigger the spread of decoys you put out, the more successful you're likely to be in attracting them.

Typically, I set my blocks with a longline in a loose "J" pattern, the far end of the line anywhere from 150 to 200 yards out and downwind of my blind, with a decoy every five yards or so. I use what are commonly called swordfish clips to affix my blocks to the mainline; they're easy to clip on and off, even when wearing mitts. While some set an anchor on the upwind end of their mainline only, I elect to anchor both ends. I'm more concerned with keeping the birds online with my blind than ensuring that my blocks swing perfectly downwind.

I establish the "hook" of the "J" about 20 yards upwind of the blind and about 20 yards offshore. In addition, I usually set out two pods of decoys about 25 yards offshore, one immediately upwind of the hook, the other 20 yards downwind from my blind. In total, I run five- or six-dozen decoys in the set. When all goes perfectly, bills trading on the open water turn upwind and follow the longline in, settling into the opening in front of my blind that lies between the hook of the "J" and the downwind pod. When birds are in groups of more than a dozen, it's not uncommon for them to not fully commit and land. Often they get a little jittery on final and swing downwind, passing in front of my blind where they offer 20- to 35-yard crossing shots. As with most divers, they're simply a little nervous whenever flying towards or over land.

While I use bluebill and canvasback decoys almost exclusively, I don't think it's absolutely necessary, especially for the pods in close. For the long line, however, the dark and white contrast of diving duck decoys does stand out on the open water and ultimately attracts bluebills and other divers more effectively than more drab dabbler blocks.

While scaup are much more accommodating when it comes to commitment than their larger and more renowned cousins, the canvasbacks and redheads, converting that opportunity into a full game bag is another matter altogether. They will quickly and consistently embarrass each and every wingshooter who believes the required lead for a bluebill is no different than that for a mallard. Bluebills have a tendency to humble all but the best and most instinctive shooters. With the exception of the canvasback, no duck on the marsh flies as fast. Further, while "cans" tend to fly in straight lines, bluebills fly in patterns roughly equivalent to what you could expect if you gave an Etch-A-Sketch to a monkey. To top it off, their penchant for

© Dean Pearson

SCAUP IN RECOVERY

Through the 1950s, '60s, '70s and early '80s, the annual USFWS waterfowl breeding population surveys pegged scaup numbers (lesser and greater scaup combined) in the traditional survey area between 4.4 million and 8 million birds, with an average annual population in excess of 6 million. A marked decline was observed in scaup numbers beginning in 1985, and the species has been on a downward trend until recent times, bottoming out at 3.2 million birds in 2006. There has been meaningful recovery in the last decade, however, with the 2016 census estimating 4.9 million scaup, right at the long-term average. The North American Waterfowl Management Plan goal for this species, benchmarked on average populations from the 1970s, is 6 million breeding birds. In the western boreal forest of northern Alberta, northern B.C., Alaska, the Yukon and the NWT, where the majority of scaup breed, the population is now one percent above the long term average. Once North America's second most populous waterfowl, as of 2016 scaup now reside in third place, an improvement from a decade ago when they were our fifth most abundant duck.

relatively low flight brings an unwelcome visual measure to your shooting prowess, or lack thereof, with your shot pattern more often than not peppering the water well behind target. Hunting bluebills, in fact, is the surest way I know of for stripping the paint off your decoys. I think it was waterfowling icon Jimmy Robinson who once offered what he called his three most important shooting tips for bluebill hunters. "Lead them a lot. Then lead them further. And finally, lead them even more yet." It's all but impossible to over-lead a scaup when he's on the swing, especially when he's got a tail wind.

GUNS AND LOADS

The scaup may not be a large duck, but they are deceptively fast fliers and notoriously difficult to put down for keeps. Whether hunted over decoys or pass shot, I've found that shot sizes 2, 3 or 4 perform best. While steel loads are more than capable when hunters keep

Bluebills are a happy-go-lucky duck, firm, plump and game to the core, with a nervous, restless nature that **keeps them flying in virtually all weather.**

their shooting ranges reasonable, bluebill hunting is one of the situations where I believe that modern tungsten-based loads earn their lofty price tags.

Seasoned scaup hunters will tell you that if you don't hit your bird with the heart of the pattern, you should expect a wounded duck. It's therefore both ethical and essential to be prepared to swat any shot bluebill that dives upon hitting the water as soon as it resurfaces for air. Even when

hunting with experienced dogs I recommend this practice, as it takes an extremely persistent retriever to track down a strong-swimming, incessantly diving bluebill that's been wing-tipped.

Because of the importance of quick follow-up shots to deal with wounded birds, I prefer and recommend semi-autos and pump-actions when hunting bills. The third shot offered by magazine guns is critical. With today's tight-patterning loads, I've found that a modified choke handles most scaup hunting scenarios effectively.

I live in central Alberta, in the heart of what many acknowledge as the best mallard hunting region of North America. Despite that, when I find time afield this

fall you can bet I'll motor out to Nettle Island once again. With any luck the weather will be a little nasty, the clouds dark, and the bluebills will dance into the teeth of an autumn squall, the west wind buffeting their sturdy bodies. From the little island I'll launch loads of chilled 3s at each flight of bills that succumbs to the spread. As always, I'll miss more than I hit. But I'll care little about my shooting percentage, for on the next gust, or perhaps the one following, another flight of bills will rocket through the blocks before rising skyward like homesick angels.

And as the western skyline turns apricot, signaling it's time to pick up for the day, I'll pity the hunter who doesn't know the feel and smell of the big water marsh, or the sight and sound of bluebills as they ride the October wind.

Kicking the Bluebird Blues

Warm, sunny and windless skies can kill a waterfowl hunt, but you can still find the ducks on those beautiful, terrible, days

BY BRAD FITZPATRICK

DUCK AND GOOSE HUNTERS develop a special glint in their eye when the forecast calls for winter to be at its worst. During those icy, windy, frigid mornings when our neighbors are dumping salt on the driveway and inventorying the refrigerator and pantry, we're gathering up our gear and whistling into the howling wind. Bad weather means good waterfowling, a day when the birds are looking for a place to drop in and willing to bite on just about any decoy spread you throw out.

But then there are other days, those windless, sunny, unseasonably warm and utterly miserable

PLAN OF ATTACK

Don't get caught off-guard by calm days. Before the temperature rises and the winds stop, you need to have an idea of where you can still find flocks.

"Birds are still creatures of habit. Even on bluebird days you have to go where the birds are," says Joe Thole of Rig'Em Right. "I set up in areas that birds are loafing or feeding in; avoid shooting areas birds are roosting in, this puts less pressure on them and helps to keep them in the area longer."

To have a handle on where the birds will be loafing and feeding, you have to get out and scout. Keep track of any areas where you find birds on calm days, and make these areas your first choice during warm, sunny periods of the season. It's also a good idea to write down where you've seen birds and record the details of the weather in a journal. By chronicling what you've seen and taking careful notes on weather conditions and duck movement you'll have a far better understanding of what's really going on in your hunting area than if you

mornings when those same neighbors are playing bag toss and firing up the grill for the first time since September. Those beautiful days that the rest of the world enjoys are terrible for a waterfowler, because even though you'll be comfortable and warm in the blind, the birds aren't moving. And even if they do fly by, they aren't buying into your frumpy little cluster of decoys

sitting stone still on the water's glass surface. Flooded timber hunters love sunny days, but for most fowlers, warm weather can be the kiss of death.

Fear not. Good weather doesn't always mean bad hunting, and there are some tricks you can employ to draw ducks in on those bluebird days. Here is how the experts bag their limits in the dead calm.

simply drove around and watched birds. Look for patterns to develop in regards to the weather and keep track of wind direction, temperature change, weather fronts, and dates.

MAKE 'EM MOVE

On a calm day, birds are more inclined to give your decoys a hard look before committing. This means you'll have to come up with a way to sell the birds on your spread, and movement is one of the best ways to accomplish that. Veteran dog trainer Tom Dokken of Oak Ridge Kennels recommends bringing along an old fishing reel spooled with a non-reflective fishing line. For his decoys, Dokken uses 40- to 50-pound Berkley FireLine and attaches it to the keel of a single decoy along with a two-pound weight.

"It doesn't take a lot of motion, but that little bit of motion can

make the difference," Dokken says. He cautions, though, that having too much line or attaching it to a bunch of decoys can create a fiasco, especially if your dog gets tied-up in the middle of a hard retrieve. Having one decoy that moves and that you

jerk rig. He also adds that having large, easy-to-see decoys that are in prime condition is important.

"Your decoys will be more visible on sunny days, so use this to your advantage," Thole says. "I am famous amongst my hunting partners for

When it's sunny and calm birds will be **spread out** and **relaxed,** not bunched tight like in cold weather.

can manage without creating a mess is a great way to lure in more birds.

Thole recommends adding movement, too, but he prefers using a jerk line like the Rig'Em Right

using the maximum number of decoys that our boat can carry, so needless to say, I like big numbers, but more importantly, clean decoys that don't have the paint flaking off,

broken heads or leaky keels. Be sure you don't have anchor lines wrapped around the necks or two or three decoys touching one another. When it's sunny and calm birds will be more spread out and relaxed rather than bunched tightly together like they tend to be during cold weather late-season hunts."

Mike Anderson of Federal Premium Ammunition is a serious waterfowler, and says that you have to mimic natural conditions closely on calm days to get the birds to buy in.

"Early season geese tend to have the same pattern during mild weather in that they roost on a big body of water and right away in the morning head straight to a field to feed," he says. "When flying out to feed they will be in family groups and tend to land and feed together."

Anderson says that the key to reeling these geese in is to provide a decoy spread they expect to see.

"When setting up your spread you want to make it as realistic as possible. Most family groups range between four to eight geese, so set your spread to make sure you don't have groups larger than that as this looks unnatural. I find myself only using 20 to 30 full-body goose decoys with three to five family groups as long as I am on the "X" in the early season."

HIDE IN PLAIN SIGHT

Bright sunshine and little wind make it easier for the ducks to spot you in the blind, so you have to be careful not to alarm approaching birds. Your goal is to keep the birds focused on your decoys and their attention off you, which means you'll need to hold still and camo up.

"On sunny, calm days ducks are much more apt to pick out a shiny face looking up, hands moving about, or a boat motor that isn't covered up," Thole says.

"Make sure you pay extra attention to detail when it comes to both your hide and what you look like from above. Another overlooked detail is sound, ducks will hear your partner when he says, 'get ready, here they come Joe Bob' or your retriever whining and moving about. All of these things are magnified without wind. Stay still, keep your face down and be as quiet as possible."

Thole also recommends keeping the sun at your back. This makes it harder for the birds to see you during their approach and puts the light in the hunter's favor. Using the sun to your advantage may make birds commit that would otherwise smell a rat and flare off at the last moment. This will require you to select a blind location that encourages the birds to approach from directly in front of the blind.

When you're scouting, make note of the direction of the sun. On a heavily overcast, windy day this is less important than on clear, calm days. Select a few blind sights that will put you in the proper position when daylight breaks.

CALM DOWN WITH THE CALL

You can get away with mediocre calling when the wind is high, but when things are calm the birds will be able to pick up on a bad tune. The best way to prevent scaring ducks with your off-beat staccato miscues is to call less and softer.

"Call very lightly; use a timber call and make sure you are only calling them on the corners," says Thole. "Just subtle quacks, leave the ringing hail call at home. The lonesome hen call is a good one to try on bluebird days."

If you've selected a location where the ducks are going to be anyway and you've got a believable spread of well-maintained decoys, heavy calling isn't required. In fact, one of the reasons you're missing ducks might be because of all your vocalization. Let the ducks work your spread, be patient

and still, and keep your calling to a minimum.

LEAVE THEM BE

Overhunting is one of the quickest ways to ruin a good blind location, and even the best areas need periodic "rest." Sometimes the best option on a dead calm day is to stay home, sleep late, and let the

birds pile up. Thole recommends giving your hunting area an occasional break, and often there's no better occasion to do so than a beautiful, calm day. As much as we'd love to spend every available minute in the blind, sometimes the best advice for long-term success is to back off and let the birds get comfortable.

DON'T CHOKE

We don't typically think of switching guns, chokes, and ammunition on sunny days, but there's value in having extra reach when the birds are working on the edge of your shooting range. On days when the sun is high, birds are more likely to flare at the first sign that your setup isn't legit, so use a choke one constriction tighter than normal. Cloudless skies mean that you'll be able to see the ducks coming from farther away, so you should be ready to take them the minute they come into range. Many hunters swear

by 3½-inch shells for longer ranges, but it's been proven the 3-inch patterns just as well if not better. Use a load designed for maximum range, like Federal's Black Cloud, which has a wad specifically designed to hold an even pattern at long distances.

The Big LOCK-UP

How one late season warrior learned to stop fearing the ice and love the deep freeze

BY DAVID DRAPER

I HEARD THE DISTINCTIVE SOUND before I saw who was responsible for it. A few steps further and I could make out the shadowy figure of my hunting partner waist-deep in the slough and surrounded by frozen water. His swinging arms were choreographed to the deep *tha-chunk* of axe meeting ice. Sometimes it pays to be late.

"Froze up, huh?"

"Yup," Jeff grunted without breaking stride. "I came out last night to take a look and she was solid right near to the fence."

Nebraska had suffered a severe cold snap and our honey hole had turned into something more suited to Hockey Town than the mallard haven it usually was.

"Ya shoulda called," I answered. "I wouldn't have slept in."

Picking up a spud bar from behind the blind, I joined Jeff on the ice and went to work doing what the Titanic couldn't—breaking ice.

Frozen water is the bane of duck hunters everywhere from about the 40th parallel north to the Arctic Circle. Even those hunters south

of 40 degrees have to contend with ice from time to time when Mother Nature scoffs at global warming. But iced-over lakes and ponds don't necessarily send ducks fleeing south, effectively ending your waterfowl season early.

It's been a decade or more since that particular ice-breaking incident and I like to think I've gotten smarter in my waterfowling pursuits. Truth is, I'm probably just lazier. Instead of swinging an axe when ice invades, I spend my time scouting, looking for any open water I can find. As long as there isn't a foot of snow covering the crop fields (and there rarely is where I live in the rain shadow of the Rockies), the smallest slough or other stream of moving water will hold ducks and geese long after the Ice Age invades.

Normally, the North Platte River stays open on its upper reaches in the Nebraska Panhandle where I do most of my waterfowling, with ice jams more common farther down the valley. Last year, was a particularly brutal one for waterfowlers here, and across the country. Winter came early and stayed late. By mid-December, sub-zero temperatures were threatening to lock up my little corner of the waterfowling world with ice inching farther upriver than had been in years.

Many of my friends are tied to that stretch of the river, and so go their fortunes. All week the talk centered on disappearing birds, with text messages flying back and forth about just where the river was freezing up and where the birds would go when it did. The more pessimistic ones were bemoaning an early end to what had been to this point a pretty good duck season. I lamented the cold with them even as I held on to hope that a secret little spring creek that would resist the coldest of cold snaps.

SEARCHING FOR SLOUGHS

Access to that short stretch of open water came about through the kind of six degrees of separation Kevin Bacon would be jealous of. Often knowing a guy who knows a guy is the best way to find hunting access. Sometimes it requires a little more hard work and lot more diesel fuel, but the rewards are worth it.

To save precious gasoline, start scouting at your desk with good topographical and aerial maps of the area, like those from Terraserver (www.terraserver.com). Google Earth also provides a duck's-eye view, revealing hidden ponds and pocket water so small conventional maps may not list them. Pay particular attention to spring creeks, warm-water sloughs and tailraces with faster moving water that stay open longer. Cooling ponds attached to power plants are usually the last refuge for birds before they're forced south and while you may not be able to hunt them, you might be able to gain access to nearby fields and catch birds as they fly out to feed. Cross-reference your finds with township and plat maps that list ownership and keep your cell phone charged.

After doing your homework, it's time to put in some windshield time driving back roads with your master map in hand. Spend most of your time on the roads in the early morning or just before sundown. Park your truck near the most likely looking areas and wait, watching the skies for ducks trading between spots. Note access points, pullouts and any other pertinent info, such

Talk centered on **disappearing birds,** with text messages flying back and forth about where the river was freezing.

as landowner names and phone numbers, on your master map. Then start dialing for ducks.

END-OF-THE-YEAR GEAR

The great thing about freeze-up is the birds aren't too picky, which is a welcome change at the end of the year after dealing with a month of decoy-shy ducks. When you're sitting on the only open water around, flocks act like flies, buzzing your spread until you almost feel like you have to swat them away.

Big rigs aren't required, especially on small water. I typically only pack in a dozen or so high-quality blocks—Avian-X is an excellent choice. These are used more to position the birds in front of me then actually attract them. I don't lean too heavily on the call either, unless I catch some high migrators that might be looking for a place to rest. Then I just get on them early, and shut things down once they start dropping. A few contented quacks on the corners and a little chatter is usually all it takes and, admittedly, those calls are probably more for my benefit than birds who are anxious to toast their feathered butts in water so warm it's steaming.

That iced-over day a decade ago, Jeff and I and our friend Mark were rewarded for the sweat equity we spent opening up a bedroom-sized hole for the ducks dropping in out of the blinding snowstorm that accompanied the cold temperatures. In less than half an hour, we had 18 ducks on ice—our limit of five mallards apiece along with bonus wigeon for each man. It was worth the hard work, even if we spent more time chopping ice than actually hunting.

This past season was a little different, and not just because I did haven't to bring along an axe. The birds were already there, having spent the night on the steaming stream. As we approached the high-banked bend in the creek before dawn, they flushed, waves of them taking wing at our interruption. It wasn't long, as in minutes, before they started flocking back, small groups of them buzzing me as I set the decoys, which, like the calling, were probably completely unnecessary. At times, ducks splashed nearly at my feet before jumping back up when they realized their error.

I'll admit it did take a little more than half an hour for Tess and me to fill our straps, but not for lack of opportunity. I blame the multiple layers of clothing it required to keep hypothermia at

bay, but more likely our shooting, like the weather, was just cold that day. Still, we managed to keep our black Lab Aengus moving as he retrieved mallards, wigeon, gadwall and even a green-wing teal, who obviously missed the memo about heading south. He enjoyed hunting more in sub-zero temps rather than the warmer days of early season and willingly, even eagerly, made multiple trips across the skinny flow.

Flowing water and some foresight in finding it can help you stop worrying and love the lock-up.

If you know where to look, some of the best duck hunting of the season can be had when everyone else thinks all the birds have disap-peared. Later that morning, from the couch next to a roaring fireplace, I texted a few friends, inquiring as to their luck with the ducks. "River's locked up," one replied. "Freezing in a field waiting for the geese instead." I sent a photo of an ice-covered dog, red-legged mallard clenched in its mouth.

"Not everything is under ice."

MOVING
VIOLAT

Breaking down a few days' duck and goose action with motion decoys

BY SKIP KNOWLES

[*Editor's note: WILDFOWL staff had the chance to hit central Kansas with Ricky Hart of Lucky Duck for a foray into using the company's latest motion spinners, swimmers and flappers. A solid hunt unfolded, a good story in its own right, and we bolstered the account of the hunt with bonus tips on the modern use of motion in the field.*]

ONS

DAY 1

Daybreak arrives over a small water puddler setup facing a fickle north wind, conditions cloudy with a little sheet ice and light snow falling. Perfect. The Super Swimmer HD worked wonders when the wind lulled, providing water movement and ripples in the spread. Ricky Hart and I scored dream limits of six drakes each by 8:40, five greenheads and a bull spring, on a killer waterhole created by Ed Markel 10 years ago, a case study in one man's vision for waterfowl property. It was originally just pasture and his friends thought him nuts for trying to create a duck hole, but Ed the engineer had ideas. Peace Creek runs through the ranch, and Ed put a dam in to create one of the

hottest holes in the area. "Now we are killing big whitetails and turkeys on the place as well, and divers on the deeper north side and puddlers on the other."

Ed's friend Mike Pierce said, "I asked him when he finished the property, 'Ed what did that first duck you shot on the new pond just cost you?'"

Ed said, "about a hundred grand . . . then I shot another and told him 'I feel better I just cut my price in half.'" The best part of the hunt was seeing Ed's dog, Cade, just 7 months old, absolutely killing it on the retrieves.

Enough pintails were flying around that once we shot our five greenheads, we decided to try for that ultimate drake limit. I had first chance at a big pintail drake and got overexcited, shot it in the butt, only to watch Ricky smack him for his ultimate limit. My next

chance came and a corn stalk stuck me in the my eye as I swung the gun. The bird was at 30 yards but I couldn't see to shoot until it was at 50 plus, but down he went. Thank you, Federal Premium high velocity 2s. . . .

SK: People know motion kills in the field. So how do you make it work in the water? What did we do so right that first day?

Hart: We had the Super Swimmer out right away, and the wind was coming and going, but we had certain birds wanting

to finish on our end of the blind. It's important to incorporate motion in the spread because it's drawing attention away from you and the blind. It creates the realism so it's not a stale simple spread. If you create movement and get it right and it's a spot that ducks want to be, you can't go wrong. We ran a split spread with decoys along that front edge in a U shape. The swimmer was upwind at the point of the spread mixed in with a few decoys to get them moving.

Generally speaking, I want to run the motion within a good visual distance of the spread and the

Always face spinners into the wind. They run better and **look more realistic.**

blind, just on the inside of a point, for example, so the birds can see the movement. Spinners are placed off to the left and right. The birds that day were wanting to slide on the outside edge of the spread, so it really worked…hunting from a pit the wind was coming over our left shoulder and to the right a bit, they wanted to sit on the outside edge.

Always face your spinning wings into the wind. It not only makes them run better but looks more realistic. Water sets, I run two to four spinners directly in front of me or off to the sides…if birds are wanting to sweep and are falling short of where it's at, I'll pull the ones in front and get them to sweep in front for good side shots at 15 to 25 yards.

I'm placing my duck decoys where I don't want the birds to land. It's like putting up a wall, even Jim Ronquest and the Hudnalls say that, "don't put the decoys in front of you because they aren't going to land right there, you want them to land to the inside edge of the decoys."

So first determine if the birds are sweeping past the spinners or coming in directly and landing near it, and work from there.

DAY 2
A bitter cold but bluebird day with no wind and the sun at our back

meant decent conditions for a small-water hunt, but this time, things were not going our way. We seemed to have picked the wrong spot on one of Hooray Ranch's top holes, the catfish ponds. Normally a home run spot, but there were other

adjacent ponds where it was clear the ducks were happier hanging out that day. Ducks would circle us too high and leave most of the time, but we still nailed a dozen or so. I whiffed on a speeding canvasback I shouldn't have shot at, and caught a huge ration of 'it' from the guys.

Revenge was sweet: The entire blind took it to the plug on a lone mallard at 20 yards, **and nobody cut a feather.**

Revenge was sweet: I sat out the next volley and enjoyed watching the entire blind take it to the plug on a lone mallard floating slowly past at 20 yards, and nobody cut a feather. They all just sat stared at each other in disbelief; Lucky Duck,

indeed! A fine moment. I was disappointed to see Randy Hill redeem himself soon after with an impossible double on a pair of screaming overhead ringnecks, one of those leaning-out-of-the-blind shots, both ducks falling stone dead on the dike behind the blind. But it was overall tough hunting at this spot, and even our Lucky Duck Super Swimmer HD (available starting this summer) seemed to surrender under a burden of ice.

SK: Day 2 was tough. Where do most people blow it on water sets with motion?

Hart: We weren't where the birds wanted to be and the sun was right at our back (good), with no wind (terrible). And, if you remember, we were standing around waiting on a few people before we started hunting, and unfortunately that's when the most bird activity occurred on that spot, right at dawn. So motion or decoys aside, there is no substitute for getting after it early and being in the right spot. Even so, we are not going to be successful every time, all you can do is analyze and ask yourself, is it the spread, lack of wind, overcalling, who knows? That's why it's called hunting. Everybody blows it. Everybody struggles.

SK: What's the smart way to use motion on the water when it's like that?

Hart: You have to consider, are you working stale birds? What's it like in the overall area? Sometimes you gotta change it up, maybe dull up the spinning wings a bit, or use an intermittent timer, and you generally should plan to turn motion off when birds are breaking down and committing. Whether it's pulling a spinner or putting one out at that point in time, when it comes to stale birds you have to tinker. The great thing about waterfowling is you never know when a fresh group of new birds will arrive, and the cool thing is quite often the stale birds will tend to break down and be triggered and start to act like the new birds, probably in competition for food. This is true for ducks, not honkers.

DAY 3
It was one of those days you still can't believe happened. An outrageous party goose shoot from an Avian-X A-frame blind after Randy Hill showed up and helped set up on a winter wheat field big flocks of lessers had jammed the evening before. Brush and grass from the hunt site hid the blinds perfectly for 10 guys crouching from a dry ditch, with three more hidden on the side in Tanglefree layouts. We finished five flocks for limits of six each, cutting a record 34 birds from one flock. That is not a typo. I had never seen so many lessers finish in big flocks. A nice birthday present for ranch manager Chad Pore. We quit by 9 a.m. after the second flock of some 1,500 birds finished to 20 yards over the 600 or more Hard Core full bodies. That afternoon we shot close to five-dozen pheasants for a perfect day.

I told Hill I'd never seen little geese finish like that, and he pointed out "Everyone thinks they are so smart, when they are actually a lot dumber than honkers, it's just that lessers need to see big numbers of decoys and nobody does that except for on snow geese," he said. "Only reason we slaughtered those geese is because we had the right spot and put out 600 full bodies."

SK: Your two Lucky Duck goose flappers worked like a charm, and we did no flagging with the wind at our back. It was clear the last group keyed right on the flappers. And finished to the right, even though the wind should have put them in the middle. How do you set up flappers for geese? Are many people buying them?

HART: Yes, that was pretty typical. For geese I use one or two goose flappers and seem to choose my right side, 10 to 20 yards off to the right, and let them run while

birds work because any time you stop motion it draws attention. If they are liking it why change anything? We just let them run. And yes, we are selling the hell out of them in Cabela's, now in their third year. It works on a 12-volt battery with a remote and on-off button and timer, and has a rheostat to adjust speed. The cool thing is ducks work very effectively over it as well.

Most of the effectiveness is because when used properly it keeps incoming birds' attention off the spread and away from your blind.

SK: Why do so many people think geese, Canadas at least, hate any kind of motion?

Hart: Hard to say. Many people don't seem to think that geese like any motion beyond a little flagging, it's true, but we are helping change that. I believe perhaps it's because geese seem to have figured out the duck spinners in a hurry, and don't often seem to like them.

DIY
Duck Ponds

There are no shortcuts to killing more birds, but if you have the fortitude, building your own greenhead honey hole is the way to go.

BY BRAD FITZPATRICK

NOT LONG AGO, A RETIRED duck hunter friend bought a small parcel of land with a lake. He was going to spend the golden years fishing for monster rock quarry bass, but soon discovered the previous owners had started a piping system to flood adjacent ag fields. Luckily for us, he wasn't married and started funneling money into a duck impoundment project that still has no end in sight.

Just before Thanksgiving we hunted together, and a lone ringneck came into one of his ponds. I didn't even think about pulling the trigger as he shot the first bird off a piece of property he had worked his butt off some 40-odd years to buy. The drake ringer is now in the hands of taxidermist Sierra Langbell, so he can remember that day and all the hard work (and hard-earned money) he has put into the place.

Honestly, the flooded corn and millet he owns isn't the duck hunting mecca all of us who get

© Dean Pearson

to throw decoys there thought it would be. Not yet. But that hasn't stopped him from pursuing the dream of creating a mallard paradise. After all, killing ducks is just a small part of it. The memories we will make with friends and family far outweigh straps full of birds.

Much of our waterfowl management stems from a century of conservation initiatives sponsored by groups of forward-thinking hunters. Waterfowl are unique because they represent a shared commodity; if things go wrong in Saskatchewan it affects hunters in Texas, so migratory birds require special attention. Most of these initiatives are large-scale objectives funded by groups like Ducks Unlimited and Delta Waterfowl.

Outfitters and corporations have been creating duck havens for years, but you (and maybe a few buddies) can carve a niche on smaller, private lands. Taking the time to renovate your property for duck hunting can be a long-term investment that pays high dividends, both financially and

in the quality and quantity of birds you harvest.

If you're thinking of building an impoundment I applaud you, but before breaking ground take a look at some of the factors involved in creating a landscape that is attractive to birds. And pay close attention to CRP and WRP enrollments that can help subsidize your new venture and create fine habitat. In some cases, state and federal governments will actually help with

grading and building levy systems. It just depends on the agency and funding availability.

THE RIGHT LOCATION

Think of your impoundment as a marketing program for waterfowl—you have to give the intended audience what they want. This will vary based upon location, the surrounding habitat, and species you're trying to woo. There's also a bit of luck involved; if your property

is located next to a large body of water that is public ground, you're in good shape. The same goes if the farmer next door is growing a couple thousand acres of rice or corn. But even out-of-the-way properties can be attractive to birds, especially in areas where waterfowl traffic and have limited options to rest.

According to Michael Porter of the Samuel Noble Roberts Foundation in Ardmore, Oklahoma, the more isolated a pond is the better the odds it will attract and hold ducks.

"However," says Porter, "ducks can learn to tolerate human activity when an impoundment is not hunted." In short, more isolated impoundments with minimal human activity will up the odds of success.

Human visitors aren't the only ones that can keep ducks away from your impoundment, Porter says in an article from *Ag News and Views*. Livestock can ruin a duck impoundment by eliminating vegetation, increasing turbidity by stirring up mud, and creating steep pond edges that make it more difficult for waterfowl to negotiate the bank. Generally speaking, cattle are the kiss of death to duck ponds, so choose an area for your impoundment where it's safely away from the chisel-edged hooves of grazing herds. If that's not an option, build a fence to keep bovines at bay.

Some pond builders, particularly those who are accustomed to building fishing ponds, have a tendency to create steep banks. This allows the pond to get deeper faster and limits the amount of aquatic plant growth that can occur near the bank. That's fine for fishing, but not ideal for waterfowl. Dabblers like pintails, wigeon, mallards and teal prefer shallow water—usually three feet or less—so if these are your primary targets, you'll need to make sure that a sizeable portion of the impoundment is shallow. You can incorporate a few trees into your pond as well for even more appeal. Tree-nesting species like wood ducks will use the area during the brooding season and mallards have a well-documented affinity for flooded timber. The downside of trees is that they are attractive to predators like hawks and raccoons, and the constant dropping of leaves and fruit can increase sedimentation and a more acidic environment which can alter plant populations. Tannins, primarily a result of leaves and acorns in the pond, create tea-colored water, and this makes the pond less desirable to ducks because it is more difficult to see forage plants below the surface.

WHAT ABOUT BLINDS...
The first few seasons, get an idea of where the ducks want to be before building a permanent blind or sinking a pit. You only want to move a 14-foot steel rectangle once—trust us. Here are few portable blinds we suggest.

MOMARSH INVISIMAN
One of our all-time favorites, the lightweight Invisi-Man can go almost anywhere, even if there's zero cover. The legs are telescoping, so you can hunt dry ground on up to 30" of water.
$300 | momarsh.com

AVIAN-X A-FRAME
The A-frame assembles in less than a minute, once you know what you're doing, and is one of the most comfortable "stow-and-go" ground blinds we've ever killed a mallard out of.
$499 | avian-x.com

Vegetation is a critical concern when creating a duck impoundment. Pond plants will serve both as a refuge and a food source for birds, so you want to be certain to have the right blend of both cover and feed to optimize success. For decades, private pond owners have been trying to eliminate cattails and other plants from the surface of pond water, but that's not necessary in a duck impoundment. That ring of cattails not only provides the birds (and hunters) with cover but it is also the veil that stands between birds and predators. Coyotes, foxes, raccoons, skunks, possums, and the myriad of other beasts that feed on ducks and duck eggs will have a much harder time navigating through a sea of cattails.

"The presence of abundant duck food plants in water is probably the most important criteria for attracting dabbling ducks," says Porter. "Clear, shallow water is generally the best approach to encourage submersed and immersed aquatic duck food plants in permanently flooded impoundments."

One of the most common questions landowners ask is how large they need to make an impoundment to draw in ducks. Even though larger impoundments are likely to attract more birds, small impoundments can bring in ducks and geese. The size of your impoundment is, quite obviously, going to be dictated by your available land and budget, but there's some good news; whether you are building the impoundment yourself or hiring an excavator, a shallow pond with gently-sloping sides is easier and faster to construct. Therefore you can often build a two-acre impoundment for about the same cost as a traditional one-acre fishing pond.

CONTROLLING WATER LEVELS

Manipulating water is the key to a quality duck hole. This can be as simple as a pipe and valve, but it's very important to have the ability to drain the impoundment during the spring and summer months to encourage the growth of native submerged plants like smart weed and sedges, and this should be done in the warmer months leading up to the season so that the water level can be increased to normal depths for hunting. Some hunters plant corn or rice, but there are also a number of blends like Five Oaks' Golden Millet and Mossy Oak BioLogic's Guide's Choice, which are generally more affordable than traditional agricultural crops.

Having the ability to draw down your impoundment is essential for routine maintenance. That drawdown period during spring/summer allows you to maintain existing structures (primarily cleaning out nest boxes), add new structure like trees, perches, and islands.

A word of warning to the new farmer—a recently-drained impoundment is like the La Brea Tar Pits for heavy machines, so if you don't have a four wheel-drive tractor that's up to the task you need to be certain that the soil is dry enough to support your machinery. Finding your expensive tractor and implement hopelessly marooned in the midst of a multi-acre swamp is frustrating, so carefully assess the

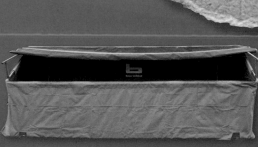

BANDED AXE
This blind can be set on the edge of the water or attach it to your boat for big-water hunts, when you're letting the pond rest.

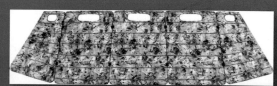

TANGLEFREE PANEL BLIND
Available in Optifade Marsh and Timber, the folks at Tanglefree can't make it any simpler to set up this fold out blind. There are also flip tops that came out last year for better concealment.

© Dean Pearson

dirt under your feet before you proceed with planting.

Planting periods depend on latitude as well as the type of plants you plan to grow in your impoundment. Corn takes a full growing season to reach maturity, so it will need to be planted during the spring. Millet should be planted so fruiting coincides with the first frost, which requires between two and three months of growth, so expect to plant them mid to late summer depending on where you hunt.

The ability to manipulate water levels in impoundments makes all of this possible, and on that note it's always a good idea to check your dam, valves, pipes, and other mechanicals when the water is low. It's usually easier and less expensive to fix equipment problems when they are detected early.

HIGH EXPECTATIONS

Will that first season be epic? That all depends on location and migration, but I'll give you fair warning. This process won't turn your backyard into Stuttgart, but it will up the odds of seeing more ducks and holding those birds.

The best way to flush all that hard work down the water pipe is over hunting. Your small impoundment isn't the only rest stop on the birds' migratory route, and they'd just as soon be huddled on a farm pond a half-mile away where they aren't being shot than dodging pellets at your place. So save your new spot for premium duck days when everyone else is fighting to launch at the public ramp.

Don't poison your new honey hole by overindulging during the first week of waterfowl season. Small impoundments should be hunted no more than once a week, says Porter, and you need to be acutely

I didn't even think about pulling the trigger as he shot the first bird off a piece of property he had worked **his butt off to buy.**

aware of how much waterfowl activity is occurring even when you're not hunting. This can be a trick because you don't want to chase committed ducks away with excess pressure, so be discreet. If you aren't seeing solid duck numbers then don't start blasting. Wait until the birds are there, hunt sparingly, and let the water rest a few days between shoots. If you do that you'll have a great hunting spot for years to come.

This is an awful lot of work to kill a few ducks and geese. But more habitat equals more ducks. And as conservationists, we have an obligation to keep populations thriving.

Chances are you'll spend more time maintaining your pond(s) than hunting them, but there's a good chance those hunts will be memorable. And as someone who has spent most of his life chasing birds on public land, I will tell you, having a little slice you can call your own, where your best friends can come to hunt—and hopefully your son or daughter can kill their first duck—is a commodity you can't put a price tag on.

For
LOVE

© Jim B. Thompson

$_{of}$ TEAL

Get ready for the Birds of September with a hot shoot on the 'littlest duck'

BY DAVID DRAPER

AS IF REFLECTED IN SOME KIND of fun-house mirror, blue- and green-winged teal, along with their trophy brother the cinnamon and the myriad of other teal species worldwide, are magnified in the minds of waterfowlers, bearing a much larger reputation than what their diminutive chassis should

project. This is especially true in the early months of autumn when special teal-only openers offer the first chance for duck hunters to get back to those marshes they've been missing since season closed so many months ago.

For a bird that tips the scales a few ounces short of a pound,

teal have an outsized following among hunters, including outdoor luminaries like Avery pro staffer Tony Vandemore of Habitat Flats, and Charlie Holder, president and CEO of Sure-Shot Game Calls. Though they live in different parts of the flyway—Vandemore in Missouri and Holder along the Texas

© Dean Pearson

coast—both men have some of the world's best waterfowling opportunities just outside their front doors, yet each get goosebumps when talking about teal hunting.

"Where other states have early goose seasons, teal are the first waterfowl I get to hunt in the state of Missouri," said Vandemore. "They're fast flying, beautiful to watch—aerial acrobats that offer fast-paced action. And because you can't hunt teal until actual sunrise, rather than the usual 30 minutes before, it adds to the overall experience. You can have that cup of coffee, watch the sun come up and listen to wind whistling through the ducks' wings. You kind of take that for granted during the regular duck season, but it's a big part of why we hunt teal."

The birds hold all the appeal for Holder, though his attraction to hunting them is the challenge the fast-fliers present, even for advanced wingshooters.

"For starters, teal are such beautiful birds, both the blue- and green-winged, even with their early-season plumage," said Holder. "Then you get the cinnamon, which is a no-brainer of a trophy if you can even find them. As beautiful as they are, teal are tough to hit and I really love the game. It's like Maverick and Goose in "Top Gun"—a pair of F-15s that stick to their wingman—and if you get to that skill level to be consistent in hitting them, mallards are no match later in the year."

GO SMALLER

To achieve that level of consistency, where you kill limits with few more than a half-dozen shells, takes practice and the aspiring teal hunter who goes into the season cold can expect to come away frustrated. Instead, a summer shooting league will do wonders for numbers of teal in the bag, especially one spent on the skeet field. A good, challenging sporting clays course will also improve the bird-to-shot ratio.

Another tip for hitting teal is downsizing. A lot of hunters show up for the opener with a blind bag full of shotgun shells left over from the last day of duck season the year before, most likely something along the lines of 2s or 4s packed into a 3-inch hull. Instead, they should stoke their shotgun with steel or non-toxic versions of light field loads in size 6 or 7½.

"Teal season and duck season are two different games," said Holder. "The secret weapon for the former is changing up your loads. A lot of avid duck hunters keep the same loads all season long, but the right ammo is a big factor for decoying teal. We've been using fives and sixes and have been really, really happy with the success of Hevi-Metal No. 6s. We haven't crippled hardly any birds since we started using that."

Vandemore's biggest tip for hitting teal?

"I shoot 1-ounce steel No. 7s," he said. "And open it up with an improved cylinder choke. Then, pick one bird, and don't flock shoot. Right before teal get over the dekes

they'll ball up then fan out. It looks like you can kill a bunch with one shot, but you really need to pick out one. That being said, with open chokes, careful what you're shooting when you get close to a limit. It's is common to hit more than one."

Teal season also gives duck hunters an excuse to break out the sub-gauge shotguns, either the 28-gauge or .410, if you can actually find steel

shells for the pop guns. Or swing a Benelli Cordoba, Browning Cirtori Superlight or other featherweight 20 gauges generally reserved for the dove fields.

"One way to have a good time is bring a hybrid dove/duck gun," said Holder. "Every year I take out some of the old salts, those local legends in the waterfowling world, and love to watch those guys pick up a .410 and take down a pair of ducks."

MIXED BAG

Early seasons for teal really offer the chance to celebrate the coming migration, much like the traditional opening day dove fete. Throughout the flyway, hunters gather together for social affairs, spending the first hours of the morning in the duck blind, followed by a day of cooking, feasting and college football. The teal flight usually departs early, and the shooting lasts maybe an hour

or two, leaving plenty of time to combine a teal hunt with other outdoor endeavors, including doves, fishing, or, along the Texas coast, an afternoon of alligator hunting.

"The tradition we have here along the Texas coast and into Louisiana is a teal and alligator combination hunt," said Holder. "Gator season typically runs that last week of September, about the same time as teal season. We'll hunt teal in

"It's about having **the right set-up, in the right place** with the right groceries."

the morning, grab a bite to eat, then run gator lines all afternoon. Last season we got 13 gators in two days, on top of a mess of teal. That's a lot of fun."

There aren't any gators in central Missouri, or none that Vandemore has come across, but he doesn't have any problem finding other fun things to do during the early teal season. Along with friends and family, Vandemore invites a few select clients to enjoy opening day.

"Every opener, we have a big breakfast before heading to the marsh," he said. "Once everybody gets done for the morning, we gather back together and pluck a bunch of bird wholes to put on the smoker. Then we fillet the breasts for Philly cheesesteaks—teal are the best tasting duck there is—and sit around eating and watching college football. It's the kickoff for waterfowl season."

You might not get an invite for Tony's signature teal Phillies, but Vandemore does provide some scouting tips on where to secure your own fresh teal for the smoker.

"I've teal hunted on every size body of water that you can think of, lakes to managed marshes, and I always try to think about what an area looks like from overhead," said Vandemore. "If you have some mud flats and real shallow water—I'm talking two to six inches, with heavy vegetation, smart weed and millet, set up in that thick stuff. You don't necessarily have to be the king of camo during teal season. That's why it's great for kids. Take a knee or a swamp seat and put your dekes in an open slash. They need to be visible. Teal are pretty inquisitive, so if they see your set, they'll often give you a screaming fly-by, what I call the burn, and then make a good tight hook and land in your spread."

As difficult as they are to hit, Holder agrees teal aren't that hard to decoy. If you're on the X.

"It's about having the right set-up, in the right place with the right groceries," said Holder. "Perfect teal

© Dean Pearson

water for us is a mature, flooded rice field. When I say mature, I mean about 30 days of water. Let that rice sit in the water until teal season. You're putting water early on it, they're used to coming to that hole. It's a magnet."

Ask a dozen different waterfowlers what his favorite duck is and you're likely to get a dozen different answers, but ask those same 12 hunters why they love hunting teal, you're all but guaranteed to get a dozen different takes on a single theme: teal are just plain fun to hunt. Though hard to hit, the aerial acrobats give hunters a chance to leave their camo at home and just go out into the marsh to have a good time before getting serious on the big birds.

SECTION TWO
GEAR

SHEETWATER
SECRETS

Do it right on skinny water and you'll make a pile of puddlers

BY NATE CORLEY

THE WHISTLE OF WINGS announced their approach: a pair of mallards, black against the overcast sky, banking toward the puddle in a low, tight circle. With wings cupped but feet hidden, the tandem buzzed the decoys and swept behind the layout blind in a rush of wind, disappearing from view. The hen could be heard chuckling eagerly from behind, but there was no need to call. These birds were coming in.

It was the final day of Washington State's marathon waterfowl season. Since mid-October, the string of Saturdays had dissolved into a blur of shotshells and feathers and alarm clocks and gas-station burritos. After four months of bird hunting blitzkrieg, the last day of January had finally arrived, and with six greenheads cooling on the mud

behind the blind, it was simply a matter of moments before the pair would reappear and the final limit completed. It was shaping up to be the perfect ending to a memorable season—one last point-blank shot to be savored, like a first kiss.

The mallards circled twice more before backpedaling over the gap in the decoys with outstretched necks. The drake was so focused on his landing he didn't notice anything out of place, not even a hunter 25 yards away sitting up to level a bead on his beak. The blast of a shotgun ripping through the mist caught his attention, though, and he rocketed skyward. His wings found the wind, and even though two more volleys were lobbed toward his tailfeathers, the bird managed to escape unscathed.

Frustration likely would have set in, but there wasn't time. Already another black dot was growing larger against the grey horizon, and it was time to regroup and reload.

The season ended 40 seconds later with a single shot and a mallard drake down face-first in the ankle-deep water: The decisive punctuation mark to signify the end of another fall.

That's the beauty of wet-field hunting. When you do it right, you can shoot a clean and efficient limit. No lost birds, no leaky waders, no hassling with a boat or trailer, just a puddle of water and a pile of ducks.

It took this duck hunter awhile to figure out how to hunt sheetwater. It wasn't for lack of opportunity or trying though. Western Washington is famous for its precipita-

tion, and after several months of Pacific drizzle, pretty much every low spot of every field around the Puget Sound is transformed into a dabbling duck's playground: six to 10 inches of water, safety from predators and usually some sort of crop to munch on.

Of course, the soggy lowland of the Pacific Northwest is the not the only region where sheetwater habitat can be found. California rice operations, Atlantic tidal flats, short-cropped pastureland near swollen Midwest rivers—even the arid fields of the Southwest can be transformed into temporary sheetwater sanctuaries for migrating mallards. And when you find these conditions, you'll need to be able to take advantage of them.

I first gained permission to hunt a sheetwater field in high school: 40 acres of puddler paradise that comprised part of a dill and cucumber farm. By mid-December, the crops had been harvested and the field plowed into bare dirt, but a foot-deep puddle the size of a basketball court had gathered near the southeast end. That's all the ducks needed. I remember glassing this field slack-jawed from the front seat of my Toyota one afternoon after school, gaping at the sight of dozens of mallards, pintails, and wigeon cavorting in the shallow water.

I returned the next morning with a sack full of decoys and a heart full of hope, but trudged back to my car empty handed and deflated. Here are some lessons learned since that first failed enterprise.

GET HIDDEN

This one is important for any manner of waterfowling, but downright essential for wet field hunts. On that first morning at the cucumber farm, I squatted behind a wire-frame blind draped in camouflage netting. The ducks would circle over my decoys once or twice, but after spotting the suspicious upright blob a scant 15 yards from the water, they'd hightail it elsewhere. No shots were fired.

A more experienced hunter would have known the value of covering up and moving the blind further from the water. When you're hunting a bare-dirt field, you can't get low enough. Digging in a layout is a great tactic, of course, but in the soupy soil of the Pacific Northwest, that usually isn't an option. To make up for this, it's a good idea to set up a minimum of 25 yards from the nearest decoy and refrain from shooting until the birds are backpedaling.

GET VISIBLE

Go ahead and test this one yourself. Next time you're scanning a wet field with your binoculars, try counting the ducks, and then re-count them. What you'll discover is that even though you'll be able to number the gaudily-plumed drakes with relative ease, you'll have a hard time picking out the hens against

the muddy background, even with the aid of high-quality optics. Female feathers are designed to fool the eyes of predators, and in a shallow puddle with plenty of lumps and clutter, this natural camouflage is remarkably effective.

Savvy sheetwater hunters will employ drake decoys exclusively in

bachelor spread assuming hidden females are relaxing nearby.

CUT THE CALLING

On that first busted hunt, my mallard call was worked harder than a referee's whistle at a Oakland Raider's game. The ducks weren't buying it.

always a concern in wet-field hunting, trumpeting your presence with a hail call is not the best way to keep prying eyes off your hide. Holding down the quacks and holding still will result in fewer ducks flaring and more ducks falling.

MAKE A SPLASH

In lieu of an abundance of calling, you'll find that an abundance of water movement is a sure-fire way to make mallards curl their wings at the sight of a sheetwater setup.

The season ended 40 seconds later with a single shot and a drake **twitching face-first** in ankle-deep water.

their sheetwater spreads. This saves valuable time during set-up and pick-up and has proven remarkably effective. I believe even sharp-eyed mallards have difficulty spotting the mud-colored hens on the ground, so they will drop in readily to a

Since then, shutting up has been proven valuable time and again. Sheetwater hunting is usually done late season in the Pacific Northwest, and January mallards are notoriously call shy. Furthermore, since maintaining concealment is almost

If the water's deep enough, a good old-fashioned jerk rig should do the trick. In most sheetwater fields, though, the water is so shallow that most of your decoys will be plowing furrows in the mud with their keels if you try to attach them to a jerk line. This is a time to get a bit more creative.

Battery-powered water-agitators by Lucky Duck, WonderDuck and Mojo (where legal) make a great option. But in Washington and

Oregon, where string-powered decoys are as high-tech as the law allows, the Kick Splash decoy by Decoy Dancer can be an effective alternative. It's basically a butt-up feeder decoy with a bright orange paddlewheel for legs. By pulling the cord, you create an eye-catching splash that gets the attention of the ducks away from your blind and onto your spread. You'll discover most mallards will finish right over the spray of this decoy, making blind placement much easier.

SLEEP IN

With some exceptions, sheetwater hunting is a mid-morning game. By December, the majority of flooded fields in the Northwest have been harvested, and the ducks that use these puddles are looking for rest and companionship more than a meal. Because of this, sheetwater hunters will typically see the most waterfowl traffic after the sun's been up for a while. For example, on that last hunt of the season in late January, I didn't slide into my layout until more than an hour after shooting light, but still finished my limit by 11 a.m. Good things come to those who sleep.

GO SMALL

When planning a set-up on a sheetwater field, it's tempting to just pick the largest pool on the property. While that may work, in most cases the biggest puddle is not always the best. More important than water depth are factors such as cover for your blind and visibility for your decoys.

For example, if the biggest water in the field is completely surrounded by a moonscape of smooth mud, it may be more effective to throw your dekes out on a smaller puddle that butts up to a ditchrow to conceal your layout. On the other hand, if that smaller puddle provides good cover for your blind but is so cluttered with vegetation that your decoys couldn't be spotted by a low-flying hawk, then it's a better idea to set up on cleaner water that allows your decoys to pop in the vision of stratospheric flocks.

You'll never find the perfect puddle, of course, but don't shy away from one simply because it's small. If there's a little soggy spot that provides the best combination of both cover for you and visibility for your spread, toss out your decoys and get ready to shoot (even if the puddle's no larger than a Volkswagen van). As long as you can get hidden and your decoys can be seen, you can shoot ducks over water of any size.

WATCH THE WIND

Nothing is more frustrating than working a flock of mallards for five minutes only to have them splash down 60 yards away on the far side of the puddle. Ducks will almost always land with the wind in their face, even if the wind is a breath that would barely flicker a candle. Determine the wind direction and set up so it's blowing over your back. If the wind shifts halfway through the hunt, pick up your layout and shift with it. You may lose 10 minutes of hunting, but you'll gain more birds at the end of the day.

★★★

By the time I'd picked up on that final January morning, a flock of wigeon were already splashing down in the small pool where seven greenheads had just gone on the strap. The whistle of wings overhead indicated that more ducks were not far behind. In a few months, the winter rains would taper off, the ducks would point their beaks northward and my puddle would evaporate. But come fall, the rain will return, and with it the ducks. We'll be waiting for them.

Pattern MASTER

How Sitka's fowl guy helped create
the perfect Timber pattern.

BY SKIP KNOWLE

THE GENTLEMEN IN OUR GROUP would hear none of getting up at 5 a.m., so we awoke at a leisurely 6 and hit the timber hole in the Argos, deep in the inky dark green-tree swamp. Jeff Watt moved through the black water with his trademark economy of motion, efficiency that comes only with many years of doing something at

an intense level. Carrying impossible amounts of gear while tending the dog, he motioned for me to hide the Argo and erect the spinners as he put out three-dozen Tanglefree flocked and foam-filled blocks, the Mojos, jerk cords and Wonder Duck slappers (paddle wheels), a wild spread I would come to call Watt's Water Park.

The boys unsheathed a brace of 20-gauge side by-sides, and Jeff pulled his Model 42 Winchester .410 out. I loaded my A400 28-gauge, a gun I was excited to try on big ducks after butchering the teal with it the year prior with lethal Hevi-Shot loads.

Zach Pedersen of Rock Road Creative, filming for Sitka, moved

with efficiency similar to Watt, doing the impossible things camera guys do—capturing the morning activity while setting up to film all day with high-tech electronic gear in waste-deep swamp water...while making a plan to be invisible.

We were out to test Sitka's new Optifade Timber pattern with Watt, one of its developers, and see if we could turn a bunch of greenheads into believers. I had butterflies, my guts feeling like a million feeding mallards sound. Not just because we would be testing the new pattern, or that I was hunting with local duck-destroyer Watt. But because I hoped to see the magic, finally. Clouds and crowds always ruined my past timber hunts, which totalled three states and 20-something days of mostly fruitless tree hunkering. The curse of clouds (a deal-killer most of the time for timber hunting, because the birds see everything on overcast days) showed up but this time it didn't matter much. Wings overhead hissed through the dawn sky as we set up. Earlier reports from Jeff, and actual birds

in the air, told me this time would be different.

The region was jammed with ducks that had stalled on migration due to warm conditions and flooding further south. We had none of the conditions we needed like true cold and clear skies, but it would not matter. Arkansas was starving for ducks, because they were all here, just east of Kansas City.

If there was someone born to hatch a timber pattern with RNT legend John Stephens, it is Watt. An independent sales rep and Sitka waterfowl athlete, he hunkered with Stephens for days on end, creating this pattern. They had the secret blessing of Jonathan Hart, Sitka founder, who decided a timber-specific pattern needed to be done, no matter how small the market. Hart decided to make it happen and seek forgiveness later. Stephens, who is part artist, part hunter, and full-time waterfowl mad scientist, worked with Watt

and took the older Optifade patterns and moved them around on the computer and changed the colors to hues of the swamp.

My first impression? I looked over at my new buddy, cranky old Don Coffey, a founder of this duck club, as we waited for shooting light. I had just smiled at him,

but now could not find him. He had vanished with the pattern. He finally turned his head and I caught his face. He had just ambled about three yards to sit on a log jam and rest his back. But he blended into the timber like tree bark.

The second impression came later, after my straps were full. I swapped the gun for a camera, and found I could move among the trees right to the edge of the spread. And stand there, and shoot photos, without the ducks noticing. With this pattern, you don't have to hump a tree, just hold still.

All suspicions about Sitka's new pattern, and my 28 gauge, were quickly confirmed. A few ducks fluttered in and it was too early to tell hens from drakes, but birds piled in from the second we got there. Three ghosted right in the hole, climbed back out, and nobody shot. I couldn't stand it and as a drake gained the treetops I pointed the little gun (it's so light, you don't really swing it) and POP! That duck folded so hard it looked like it never had wings or a head and neck. *Pa-BLOOSH* into the water. Four drakes in four shots, another tree-topper and two in the hole, no cripples. Hevi-Shot is just nasty.

So this was real timber hunting. Finally. What freaked me out that first day were the outrageous lines of birds in the sky, far more than all my other timber hunts combined, sometimes four or five lines going opposite directions, and non-stop crossing singles and doubles. By no means did they all work, but enough peeled off our group tagged out by mid-morning.

Fifteen out of 16 ducks on the day were believers in the new Sitka Timber. The 16th had no idea what hit him.

WATT'S WORLD
The hunting for the next few days was intense, like everything in Jeff Watt's world. Sitka was founded when backcountry bad-asses Jonathan Hart and Jason Hairston got fed up that they had to throw crappy camo over high-tech gear by companies like Mountain Hardware, Patagonia and Arcteryx in order

to survive the alpine extremes and do what core big game hunters do. Why was nobody building gear for the original extreme athletes, hunters?

Many brands were building clothing for mountaineering, a tiny market, but not for hunting world. Big game stuff came first with Sitka, and when they launched a pricey waterfowl line of high-tech gear, the duo forged a niche that did not exist prior. Turns out hunters like comfortable, warm, dry, breathable, clothing that moves with your body and performs under all condition.

Predictably, Nancy-boys the world over groaned how Sitka gear would never sell at such a high price point…and in about one year the brand became a status symbol for core waterfowlers, particularly the

younger guns, and anybody who regularly hunted outside a cozy, heated blind.

"We have taken this waterfowl industry by storm and made waves," Watt says. "We are committed to the waterfowl game like no other. Timber is specifically for the oldest tiny niche of waterfowling, the flooded timber hunter, and nobody else is doing it. It will work in pits because it's darker and in river bottoms, too, sure, but the states of Arkansas, Mississippi, and Louisiana are our target for the pattern. We are trying to promote timber hunting and the history and the lore of it…you know what it means to the older guys. There is just nothing better in the world than watching mallards work down through the trees.

"The **jerk cord is such a key** to this kinda hunting," Watt says. "It sucks them in so much."

"It's a small market and we know it, but we don't care, because it is important."

Sound like a religious fanatic? Yeah. Guilty.

"It's a darker environment," says Jim Saubier, Sitka's waterfowl product development guru. "We did a lot of research to make sure we are meeting the 'science of concealment' promise to fool the birds, as they work in really close. Waterfowlers have un-met needs and we want to deliver on that."

'Science of concealment' is the Optifade camo pattern trademark, rooted in the idea of creating visual confusion based on how animals see, not how hunters see.

I know what I'd seen after a few days in the swamp with Watt. Finally, a proper lights-out timber hunt and all the magic involved. But what I really came to appreciate was Mr. Watt. We had been on an epic-terrible hunt together in the past, one of my many failed timber trips (some readers may remember "The Slump" editor letter) and along with all this smoking barrels and flying feathers redemption, I got a real good insight into the man.

Watt is a face for Sitka waterfowling, but will quickly tell you, "There is no single face of the company when it comes to product lines. We don't do that. Our key is authenticity. And relationships, and hard-core use in development of these products. We just wanna help build the best product and won't bring it out until it is the best, period."

So what makes the man tick? Leadership. Tightly wound, competitive, aggressive, sure, but a born leader. Riding in his monster truck on the way to duck camp, I listen to him telling his sons on the phone to get it together and rally for an upcoming Arkansas hunt, a convo that is tense at first, a bit bossy, but ending in loving laughs. Classic Jeff: He is a firebrand of intensity...as a father with sons who live to hunt, he stays focused on the good stuff, including a youngest son who is freaking out to hunt ducks in the trees. What a lucky kid, to have this guy for a Pa. A dad who keeps two great retrievers in his office... and moves a jerk cord like a Latin dance move, the marquis ensemble of Watt's Water Carnival.

When Jeff works the jerk rig, the decoys moving in sync, half-spinning, then swimming, spinning back and swimming back again, it will hypnotize you just as it does the ducks. His buddies call them The Four Tops, out there dancing in harmony. If you are old enough to get that reference and are still hunting, God bless you.

The jerk rig is a fitting metaphor for Watt, who always has his ducks in a row.

"The jerk cord is such a key to this kinda hunting," Watt says. "It sucks them in so much." When he sees the ducks coming over he pulls the Rig'Em Right cord up tight, and as they get close he lets it go so they swim slowly back, nothing jerky or fake about the motion. Murder.

THE BEST OF MO

Born in Kansas City in 1965, Watt moved to southern California at age 2 and then back to the M-O in 1981. With his water park, jerk cord, decoy spread and a buddy behind every tree, he is in heaven in the timber. Missouri is overall underrated, he believes.

"I live in the best area for timber hunting in the country," he says. "If you hit it, it is better than anywhere."

Watt has hunted the same place since 1983, and became an owner

in the early '90s. Shadow Oaks is one of the only flooded timber spots left in the Four Rivers region most years. Timber hunting was great in the area, then most of the trees died from flooding. It's between the Four Rivers refuge pools and the Four Rivers public shooting area, with the Osage River on one side and the Marais des Cygnes River on the other.

A former competitive caller, Watt is also a core big game hunter who does everything at the highest level. He has a garage full of bull elk horns and has killed four mule deer over 200 inches. He loves long range shooting and routinely tags out at 500 to 1,000 yards. Been there, shot that. Even when he fishes, it's for giant wild steelhead on the famed Dean River (like 10 times), with spey rods. The varsity stuff.

So why the timber mallard addiction? What is his deal with ducks?

"Big game hunting? I love it, but it's one shot, that's it. A 180-inch whitetail is a cool tough trophy to get, but boring as hell. Sitting in a tree waiting for one to walk by," he says. "Greenheads, well you can call ducks, and they respond and the whole thing is social. How much fun was it out there with Danny and Don today? You can bust someone's chops for shooting a hen and zing 'em for $20. And there's so much more shooting."

Driving in his giant F350, Watt's phone rings one call after the other, and I recognize the names: duck hunting dignitaries. He is non-stop advising friends like Stephens on their marketing strategies and contacts, relative to sales in stores. And hunting reports. Always hunting reports.

Broad shouldered and gray-haired with a shaved head and Fu Manchu mustache, he is an athletic sort of stocky and looks like he probably owns a Harley. He is in fact terrified of motorcycles. His brain is formidable. He finally gets off the phone and picks right up on a deep conversation we had going 20 minutes prior, right where we left off. Mine does not work that way, and he has to re-acquaint me with the subject. He must be one of the busiest fellows on earth, and the ostentatious truck is because he is always hauling tractors, boats and pro-barbecue gear.

Yes, he somehow makes time for competition barbecue "because I just like to see a lot of happy people having a good time enjoying good food..." A video of his huge booth at a cooking event shows a few hundred people drinking and dancing around his grill.

GREENHEAD OLYMPICS

As a Sitka rep and nut-job hunter, he always loved the Optifade Marsh pattern, but recognized its short-comings.

"It works well in timber in the sunlight, which is when you really want to be hunting timber, but when it's overcast, you stand out like an ear of corn in a bowl of fudge batter," he said.

With a black-smeared face and new Timber pattern, we felt like ninjas in the swamp. The final morning mallards tried to land on us as we put the decoys out, and we were done hunting in less time that it took to wade in. How can a 30-minute hunt be so cool? We carefully chose our shots and still, it was over so fast. I folded four greenheads in four shots with the 28 for a too-fast limit; no skillful feat, as the birds were hanging piñatas at 20 yards. Some days the limits just seem cruel. We stayed a bit and watched ducks land in the big open timber hole. Not his favorite spot. Jeff prefers the tighter tree holes so the birds have to do everything they can to get down and in. The hardest way, of course.

But for all the aggressive approach to life, he's fundamentally a nice guy, always bent on taking the high road (except for jokes... the dirtier the better). Those two qualities—aggressive and nice—are rarely found together. Club founder Don Coffey talks about when Jeff was young, he would pull up to the duck club late at night and sleep in the cold outside in his truck rather than come in and wake up the older guys with his arrival.

From his high-tech truck that is a travelling press conference to

his aspirational level of hunting to his competition barbecuing to his outrageous duck blind builds and big-time big-game hunts, all of it, anything in life that's worth doing, I don't know if I've ever seen someone outside of the Olympics who does everything at Jeff's level.

"You just don't do anything half-assed, do you Watt?" I ask him.

"You know, I'm surprised you'd even ask that," he replies, feigning hurt with a look that implies what-is-wrong-with-you. "I don't screw around. Do it right and be done with it."

His work with Optifade Timber seems to fit right in that...pattern.

Duck Calling's ROOTS

A few pieces of metal and wood sparked a North American obsession that still plays out on the stage at Stuttgart every Thanksgiving

BY JOHN M. TAYLOR

Dudley "Dud" Faulk (foreground) and his father Clarence "Patin" Faulk.

F. A. Allen,
Charles Ditto,
a Grubbs model,
and an early Olt.

DAN HAD ABOUT CALLED HIS throat raw. The geese were easy to call, but ducks, they just didn't want to listen. *If I only had one of those calls like the man who came down with Mr. Marshall Field had, I could reach out and get their attention,* he thought.

Dan Brown was the chief paddler or guide at the exclusive Chicago Millionaires' Club, as the locals around Olive Branch, Ill., called it. Lots of the big-shot businessmen from Chicago and St. Louis had developed a piece of land just off the Mississippi River in southern Illinois into a palatial hunting club. They had concrete-bottomed ponds to hold birds, and the best callers and guides in the area. Dan had come up from Mississippi to work, and enjoyed paddlin' for the rich sports. One of them, a guest of department-store owner Marshall

Field, had a duck call, and Dan made sure he got a good look at it. It had two pieces of wood with a metal reed in between, held together with a metal band.

Dan found a good piece of wood, split it in half, then hollowed out both sides. He found a piece of brass and carefully filed it thin, put it between the wooden halves and wrapped it in string. The end of Mr. Marshall Field's factory-made call had a cone-shaped metal piece at the end, so Dan took a piece of cow horn and made a little bell at the end to be sure the ducks could really hear it.

Dan's call was a copy of Elam Fisher's, the first duck call issued a patent by the U.S. Patent Office in 1870. Although Fisher's patent dated to 1870, there is evidence this style of call was in use in Eng-

A Chien Caille by Mervis Saltzman, the Faulk "Black Label," and a Cedar Cane by Allen Airhart.

An early D2 Regular Duck Call, a pair of Olt Perfect models.

land before then, as these "tongue pincher-style" calls have been found in English gunning boxes dating to the 1850s. Anyone who has ever blown one will understand the term "tongue pincher" that comes from the sympathetic vibration set up by the reed that causes an electric-like shock to the user's tongue. Although tongue-pincher calls provided a faint quack-like sound, they really didn't provide a good, loud mallard-duck quack.

MIDWEST INVENTION

Call development took place primarily along the Mississippi River and one of its main tributaries, the Illinois River. It was from here callmakers like F. A. Allen, Charles Ditto, August Kuhlemeier, C.W. Grubb and Charles Henry Perdew began making calls and marketing them through sporting magazines such as *American Field* and catalogs of the day like *Abercrombie & Fitch* and the Chicago hardware firm of Hibbard, Spencer, Bartlett & Co. Ditto used a gutta-percha—an early form of hard rubber—reed held into a curved insert or tone channel and a wedge. Allen used the same setup but his had a metal reed. Fred Allen also made ingenious "Bow Facing Oars" that enabled the rower to face in the direction he was traveling,

The early Hambone by H. C. Amaden, Jake Gartner, a pair of D. M. "Chick" Major calls and far right, the Mrs. Sophie Major.

allowing him to powerfully pull on the oars mechanically rigged to push back. His duck calls were often advertised alongside his patented oars.

If credit for the modern duck call can be given to one person it would have to be Philip Sanford Olt. Olt lived in Pekin, Ill., about half way down the Illinois River. In 1904, Olt marketed his first call the B-4 Adjustable, which used a small metal slide that rested atop the reed. By moving it forward and back the user could lengthen or shorten the reed, lowering or raising the pitch of the call. By far, Olt's most famous duck call was the D-2 Regular Duck Call, about which some folklore swirls. The earliest D-2s had a round exhaust hole in their insert. In 1939, the exhaust hole was changed to a "keyhole," that had a flat, square trough at

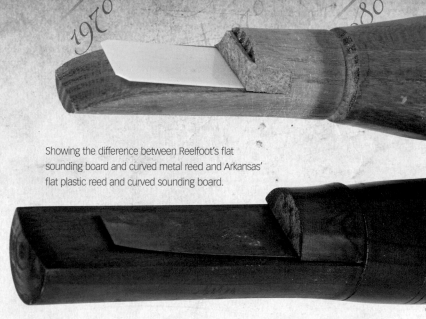

Showing the difference between Reelfoot's flat sounding board and curved metal reed and Arkansas' flat plastic reed and curved sounding board.

the bottom. Thought to be many things, the truth was the flat slot was simply a different mold-release technique that made it easier to release the insert following molding. Later, Olt returned to the original round opening, and his ancestors finally reintroduced the "keyhole" insert due to customer demand.

Perhaps the most endearing part of the D-2 was that the hard rubber from which it was made was easily filed and shaped, so that the user could customize his call to his hunting. Soon cut-down Olt calls became famous in the

A Tom Turpin by R. L. Melanson, an Earl Dennison, and a BenJon made from Perry Hooker parts.

hardwood bottoms and flooded timber of Arkansas. Although Olt is no longer in business, versions of their D-2 abound in the form of cut-downs and a reworking of the basic call by many contemporary makers.

One legendary Arkansas guide was the late Maurice Eason, who for many years was the manager and chief guide at the palatial and very private Wingmead near Roe, Ark. Eason used an out-of-the-box Olt D-2, changing the reed and cork every day or two. He had a sharp, detached style of calling. Eason said, "When I was 15 or 16, I started guiding. I got $7.50 to carry (guide) hunters and $10 if they got their limit. The extra $2.50 meant a lot to my family, so I learned very early what called ducks and what didn't."

In the flooded timber where he guided, the smooth contest stage-style of calling runs together, but Eason's "sharp" or detached style of calling sounded just like a live hen mallard sounding off, and brought ducks by the dozens.

'BO-DOCK' EVOLUTION

Up and down the Mississippi River, the Olt was copied. In Arkansas, they became wood, made primarily of Bois d'Arc (bow wood or hedge), called colloquially "bo-dock," from fence posts sunk by railroads in the late 1800s and early 1900s. The top portion produced yellow-colored calls, while the area near the base that became wet then dried produced green-colored calls, and the bottom

calls with them, and the resourceful Cajun guides copied them using native materials. Cane that grew wild in the marsh reinforced with the brass head of a fired shotgun shell formed the barrel and insert. The back of an Ace double-sided comb was filed and sanded to a thin taper for the reed, and the tone channel was set with a slight twist and the reed held in place with a wedge of cork from a fishing bobber. The

Southwest Louisiana." Sitting across his work bench, I once told Dud I wanted a Black Label, and he said, "Dat call give you hell boy," more than suggesting it was difficult to learn to blow. It was quirky, but I killed a lot of ducks with it. Names like Florine "Pie" Champaign, Noah Schexnider or Allen Airhart's Cajun Calls represent some of the old Louisiana callmakers, with Faulk and Haydels still producing great calls in the Louisiana style.

Eason's "sharp" or detached style of calling sounded just like a **live hen mallard sounding off,** and brought ducks by the dozens.

section that was in the ground gave a rich brown color to the call. Bois d'Arc is becoming difficult to obtain, and most makers no longer produce these prized calls.

As sportsmen traveled to Louisiana to hunt, they took their Olt and other

late Eli Haydel told me, "Cajuns can't grunt into a call, so they twist the tone channel to give the call the rasp." Clarence "Patin" and his son Dudley "Dud" Faulk made a special Black Label cane call "For Guides in

Another historic call was the metal-reed Reelfoot-style call. As much as these large metal-reed calls are associated with northwest Tennessee and the great duck-hunting culture of Reelfoot Lake, they actually originated in Illinois. Victor Glodo was born and raised in southwestern Illinois near Grand Tower. He was a jack of all trades: carpentry, blacksmithing, market hunting and making duck calls. When the area around Grand

The Broadbill Call

PATENT NUMBER 1176818

MAILED ANYWHERE IN U. S. ON RECEIPT OF $1.00, IF YOUR DEALER DOES NOT HANDLE

N. C. HANSEN CO.,   Zimmerman, Minn., U.S.A

Hansen Broadbill, the Dan Brown handmade, and a Red Duck

Tower was drained for farming, Glodo and wife Vada moved to Starve Island on Reelfoot Lake. Glodo's calls were all hand-made with little machining involved. They constituted a large wooden barrel into which set a flat tone board with a curved metal reed held in place with a wooden wedge that sealed the call. Glodo's calls were frequently checkered with a wide skip-line pattern, and have become the basis for all metal-reed calls. Others like John "Sundown" Cochran, John "Son of Sundown" Cochran, Earl Dennison and Johnny Marsh continued Glodo's legacy, and today there are numerous custom callmakers and descendants of these early callmakers dedicated to crafting metal-reeds.

Hunting on Reelfoot is extremely competitive with numerous blinds vying for high-flying flocks of mallards, hence the long, high-pitched "Reelfoot highballs" and other calls that use the metal-reed calls to their maximum. Reelfoot guides can really scream on these metal-reed calls. Callmaker Greg Hood once said, "Those ducks can see everything up there. The first one to attract their attention has the best chance of getting them in."

STAGE PRESENCE

Contests have done more to raise the level of calls and calling than any other activity. At one time, fine mallard calls came almost exclusively from the Stuttgart area, and good metal-reed calls came from northwest Tennessee around Reelfoot. In the 1980s, word began to spread, and a surge in callmakers and good calling resulted.

The goal, of course, is the Main-Street stage in Stuttgart where on the Saturday following Thanksgiving, the World's Duck Calling Championship is contested. The first was in 1936 with a $6 hunting coat as the prize. Early winners were from along the Mississippi from Louisiana to Illinois and Iowa. The first man to win was Thomas E. Walsh of Greenville, Miss., who called "by mouth" making all the duck sounds vocally. Normally thought to be a "man's contest," Pat Peacock Johnson, renowned callmaker D. M. "Chick" Major's step daughter, won the World in both 1955 and '56. In those days competitors used wooden calls, often their hunting call, but today callers compete with acrylics capable of drowning out a 747 at takeoff.

Duck calling is a unique American folk art form of both the calls and hunters using them to lure ducks to their decoys. In South America, guides use calls that at best make a dusky quack, relying instead on whistles made from wood or the heads of spent shotgun shells. In Europe calls are sold in gun shops, but mostly as a novelty. Here in the U.S., we are deadly serious about our calling, as it should be. It was here that the call was first formed and has now become a nationwide phenomena, sounding the clarion call to ducks across North America, just like Dan Brown wished.

Finding Your Swing

Get to the range for your pre-season shooting tune-up and be ready for the big show

BY JOE GENZEL

WITH A LIMIT OF MALLARDS IN the bag, it was time to start picking out bonus ducks. The bright mid-morning sun shined in our faces when my buddy made out the distinguished tail feathers of a fat bull sprig and let me take the shot.

I stood up and folded the gorgeous pintail. The tall bird made a distinctive splat in the shallows just in front of our stick blind. It was one of a handful of great shots (there were plenty of misses too) from last season, one I would have never made without countless trips to the skeet range. I'm a firm believer any waterfowler, especially newbies, that don't chase these little orange Frisbees in the spring and summer, are not maximizing their shotgunning potential. With somewhat small bag limits here in the U.S., it's advantageous to shoot skeet and sporting clays as much as possible. The Krieghoff guys might give a few odd looks when you pull out a Super Black Eagle II in Realtree Max-4, but pay them no mind. You're there to become a better shot with a duck gun—bottom line.

SCHOOL DAYS

First and foremost, find a teacher. "My dad had a really good friend who was a world-class trap shooter," said Craig Boddington of *Petersen's Hunting*. "So when I really got into shotguns, that's who he turned me over to."

OK, you may not have the same access as one of the greatest hunters to ever walk the planet, but the process is pretty simple: Pick out the best shot in your group of buddies and hit the range. If that's not an option, just go to the local club and ask around. I guarantee one of the white hairs will be happy to help. Just be sure you are learning from an accomplished shooter. Plenty of guys will try and instruct you, but watch them shoot before taking any advice.

FITTING IN

A wise old editor once told me: "Find a shotgun you shoot well, and then never let it go." I've shot plenty of semi-autos and double guns, but never purchased one until I knew it was the right fit. Every gun has a different feel, and there are endless options, like comb, length of pull, barrel

When I'm shooting well it's because I find the bird's beak, swing through it, and pull the trigger.

length…the list goes on. So, shoot a variety of shotguns to get a feel for what's best. My first two rounds of skeet ever were with an ill-fitting auto-loader, yielding 10 clays total, a horrid and depressing experience. I grabbed a friend's slightly hump-backed Beretta A390 and jumped to a 17 on round three, and after a few months with more trigger time, bought one.

EYE DOMINANCE

I grew up playing all kinds of sports right-handed. When my dad taught me to shoot, neither of us considered I might be left-eye dominant. We simply didn't know any better. Two years ago I was having trouble with crossing shots at a sporting clays course, when one of the instructors asked me if I had ever tested my eye dominance. "Uh, no sir," I said. He had me interlock my hands to form a circle, focusing on

an orange cone, then pull towards my face. This quickly revealed that my left eye was dominant, despite my right-handedness.

Yep, I had been shooting improperly for 20-plus years. So, I switched to shooting left-handed and it has made some improvement. It was most helpful, because I'm now somewhat ambidextrous, and can shoot birds righty in a pinch. Cross dominance doesn't require you to switch hands, but some people simply can't make the transition. There are multiple remedies, including sights, taping your safety glasses over the dominant eye and keeping the dominant eye closed.

RANGE RAT

Seasoned shotgunners may just need a few summer tune-ups, but you greenhorns are going to want to hit the range every week if possible. Beginning skeet shooters should plant themselves at station one. The bird is thrown from behind, and though it's not a typical shot you will make on ducks or geese, it is the easiest on the course and a confidence builder. I started with a high gun (already mounted to my shoulder), bringing my cheek to the stock once the clay was thrown, and graduated to cradling the stock in my armpit. You can try low gun too, which is more in line with shooting live birds. But don't move on until you're

consistently breaking at station one, and repeat the process at each spot. Also, it is generally agreed that shooting sporting clays is far superior to skeet or trap for becoming a good field shot, though any shooting practice is helpful.

FOLLOW THROUGH

The key to consistently breaking clays and killing birds is keeping the barrel moving, and your cheek on the stock. I liken it to the golf swing. You don't come to a stop upon striking a Titleist, or make proper contact if you take your eye off the ball. The same is true for clay birds. Keep the barrel moving through the shot and your face firmly planted on the stock. Your eyes should be focused on the front edge of the bird and for me personally, the open space in front. When I'm shooting well it's because I find the bird's beak, swing through it, and pull the trigger. Lead varies on speedy migrators, like teal and dove, and it's smart to take advantage of those early seasons. Then, pulling up on mallards and Canadas will feel like slow motion.

"It becomes second nature, and you don't even think about what you are doing," said Jim McConville, *WILDFOWL's* national sales manager. "You rely on instincts. I don't know when I realized that I was pretty proficient with a shotgun, but I worked very hard at becoming a good shot."

FINAL EXAM

After several months, I became an average skeet shooter, consistently breaking 17-18 per round. That gave me some confidence. But there's a difference between yelling, "pull" and knowing the right time to "take'em." Shooting any clay bird is very reactionary, but when you're in a blind it's more of a waiting game. My biggest mistake was thinking birds were in the kill zone, and shooting too soon. I was getting too excited and calling shots at 40 yards, missing because the ducks were beyond the edge of the decoys. Once you think the birds are in range, take a deep breath before opening up to suck them in a bit closer. Also, clay shooting is pretty predictable and waterfowl flight patterns are certainly not. You're going to be taking shots from different angles, in full duck gear, from a blind—completely opposite from skeet shooting in shorts and sandals. So, there's going to be an adjustment. But remember the range work, stick to the basics and you will have more good days than bad.

SECTION THREE
DOGS

BORN

TO HUNT

IMAGES BY MATT McCORMICK

MAYBE IT WAS A SMELLY OLD CHESSY, OR A CUTE-as-hell white Lab pup that once wrestled your kids and looked like a baby polar bear. Or a semi-spastic golden that somehow got the job done with outrageous vigor. It could have been a poorly-performing chocolate that would kill itself trying and was a total sweetheart.

Or maybe just your first gun dog, and that's enough.

But somewhere, somehow, a retriever at some point sunk its canines deep in your heart.

Maybe it was not a great dog, but just happened to bear witness to a happy era in your own lifetime: Your personal good old days of hunting, a time when year after year you really got into the birds. Sometimes a dog will nail you in the heart when you are in a lonely place. Perhaps its growth is associated with that of your children's, their wonder years.

Or maybe, just maybe, you are one of the lucky few who happened upon a pure thoroughbred, a bird-fetching machine, one of those tremendous canines that are simply a pleasure to be around and make you glow with pride, make you look like a good trainer when you knew the truth, you just needed to get out of the way.

Whatever the circumstance, only a hunter understands the true potential a relationship with a canine can hold.

They are born to hunt, and so are you. Those who don't live this can't understand it. Any dog can be a man's best friend. But a hunter who has spent years in the field over the course of a good gun dog's lifetime has the deepest relationship with a retriever, with the exception perhaps only of rescue and police dog owners. The hunter and his partner become more like a couple old war buddies who have seen a lot of action together.

It runs much deeper than the vacuous term "pet." Much talk in this magazine centers on "dog owners." But we all know who-owns-who in the end. Here's to our most loyal field companions, and a photo essay that celebrates their existence.

—*Skip Knowles*

BORN TO HUNT

BORN TO HUNT

Season's Just Begun

Hunt trials can fully develop your duck dog while making you a better handler. Best of all; they're fun. By Tom Dokken

THE MAIN PROBLEM with most duck dogs is their owners think training is a seasonal, part-time duty. Granted, how much time you can devote to training depends on an awful lot of circumstances, but there is no doubt a year-round approach is better than cramming in a refresher course each pre-season.

This is something I realized in the early 1970s when I started training hunting dogs. Although I felt like I could do a solid job on my own, I also made the decision to start running my dogs in AKC field trials. The competition was enjoyable and the benefits reached well beyond winning a ribbon.

For starters, simply joining the world of field trials meant advice from trainers of all skill levels who were willing to help me as a handler. Sure, there were other amateurs, but there were also several professional trainers involved. There is no substitute for experience, and many of the folks that I met in those early years had plenty of it and offered me invaluable advice. Because of that, I also joined a training club, which created further learning opportunities.

In addition to a wealth of knowledge through access to those in-the-know, my formative years running field trials helped me establish a year-round training approach, which keeps my dogs tack-sharp all year long. This is especially true given the way the original field trials have evolved from an uber-competitive climate that didn't closely emulate hunting scenarios, to today's hunt tests that demand skills all duck dogs should posses.

TESTING OUT

A quick Internet search will reveal organizations like the Hunting Retriever Club (HRC), the North American Hunting Retriever Association (NAHRA), or the AKC and their various hunting tests.

All were developed with the intention of bringing hunt tests to the masses, and they do just that. AKC field trials are also available, but for the beginner it's best to go with a hunt test.

These are offered with varying degrees of difficulty, however before signing up I highly recommend visiting a hunt test for a day to see how they operate. Knowing ahead of time what you're getting into, and what you're getting your dog into, can alleviate some of the stress of starting out and allow you the chance to truly evaluate whether you're ready to get involved.

Provided you play witness to one of these events and decide you'd like to give them a shot, it's best to start with the easiest level available. Each organization will

One benefit of hunt tests, aside from competing alongside trainers of all skill levels, is you'll get to observe multiple breeds working, many of which were blessed with exceptional genetics.

offer different levels of difficulty that may start out as simple as marked, single retrieves and end up as difficult as multiple blind retrieves that involve hand signals and honoring. In other words, everything you really want your duck dog to master will be covered at some point.

In hunt tests, your dog competes against a set standard. This removes much of the one-on-one competition, and has made the process much more enjoyable for a lot of the participating handlers. This system results in dogs that pass, and dogs that don't; you're not trying to beat other handlers and their dogs.

It's important to note that even the easy levels, might not be *that* easy right away. New experiences for our dogs come with some stress and it's not uncommon for dogs to fall a bit short during their inaugural runs. It's also necessary to say that if your dog doesn't have basic obedience skills mastered or hasn't been gunfire- or water-introduced, you should hold off until your dog is ready. Competitions are a great way to build from a solid foundation of skills, but not a place to start from scratch with a puppy or inexperienced hunter.

BREED EXPOSURE

Once you get yourself established in these hunt tests you'll probably notice the motivation to train has increased. And there will be plenty of new friends to chat with about all things dog. I've developed some great relationships, and am still friends to this day with guys I met at my first field trials. We share duck honey holes when the flights are on, an unexpected benefit.

On top of potentially gaining some hunting buddies, you'll also be exposed to a wide range of dog breeds. While some hunters lock on to a specific breed and won't waver their entire lives, others keep a more open mind. This exposure can give you some options for a future puppy.

Take note of the breeding as well. I'm a big proponent of quality bloodlines for all hunting dogs, and as you spend more time competing you'll get to witness some truly exceptional dogs work. Odds are those dogs posses superior genes, which is easier to understand after watching with your own two eyes what good genetics can foster. This is one of the reasons I always research bloodlines for generations of dogs that hold the highest titles available in hunt tests. Their puppies will be—almost without fail — smarter, easier to train, and better hunters. Seeing this firsthand is a great experience for any dog owner and waterfowl lover.

STILL NOT CONVINCED?

I don't fault anyone for being skeptical of a hunt test, whether it's an informal snowbound adventure held in the middle of winter or a more formal event conducted with open water and very realistic situations. Hunt tests often get lumped into the "show competition" category, and that can be off-putting to duck dog owners who have no desire to join that scene.

But hunt tests are nothing like dog shows, and there is nothing to fear in that realm. I've been to a pile of hunt tests over the years and the camaraderie is nothing short of extraordinary, and rarely is there ever any elitist feel to any of it (and if there is that is usually squashed pretty quickly). It truly is an environment where the dogs get to learn how to use their skills (and develop new skills) while under pressure, and you as a handler get to soak up a pile of benefits from like-minded individuals.

Hunt tests really are win-win for handler and hound.

In other words, everything you really want your **duck dog to master** will be covered at some point.

Two Birds Down

Marking doubles is hard enough. Get your dog ready for multiple retrieves with these drills. By Tom Dokken

GOOD DUCK DOGS need to know how to count—at least to two, anyway. Eventually, they should be able to count to three, but that's fodder for a different column. Most retriever owners recognize the need for their dogs to be able to successfully retrieve a double, but some fall short in their training.

If you're eyeing up a few drills to help your dog master doubles, take a long hard look at his single retrieves. Any dog expected to graduate to doubles needs to flawlessly handle single retrieves. If your dog's game is a bit off when chasing down a solo dummy, it's going to be a disaster when you introduce another. All of the obedience necessities need to be rock solid, as does the entire process of retrieving a single to hand before you consider going for doubles.

If, however, your dog possesses the foundation of perfect single retrieves on land and in the water, then it's definitely time to prepare him for making multiple retrieves.

A SIMPLE 180

As with all my drills, the first lesson concerning doubles is very simple to master. This drill requires two highly-visible dummies and a mowed lawn, and is designed to encourage memory development. With the dog at heel, I'll throw a dummy a short distance to my right. Then, I toss the second dummy to my left.

The reason for tossing the dummies in completely opposite directions is to encourage the dog to retrieve the first dummy and return to me before he thinks about the second. After tossing the dummies, I'll send the dog to the last dummy first and call him to hand. If he returns the dummy to me correctly, he gets sent in the opposite direction to retrieve the first dummy. It's imperative this stage of the process be simple and the dog can easily see the dummies. Success breeds confidence, which

comes in handy as we increase the difficulty.

If your dog seems to have any problems with this initial 180 drill, you may need to employ a check cord. No matter what, he should not be running to the second dummy until he has brought you the first. This drill, although simple, should be conducted daily for a week or so until it's easy for your dog to accomplish. If your dog gets it quickly in the backyard, feel free to change locations, but always remember to keep it easy

> If your dog's game is a bit off when chasing down a solo, **it's going to be a disaster** when you introduce an extra dummy.

enough to encourage success. This is not the time to test your dog.

COLLAPSE THE ANGLE
After mastering the 180 drill, I like to stay in the backyard and throw the dummies 45 degrees apart. This allows the dog to see both dummies, so don't be surprised if there is some hesitation or obedience issues at the onset. Again, encourage the dog to retrieve the last dummy first, and then retrieve the first-thrown dummy on memory.

If the 45-degree drill comes along nicely, I like to add a thrower into the mix provided the dog has previous experience with a handler and a thrower. If so, have your thrower get the dog's attention and then toss the dummy. Once it's tossed, you should then throw your dummy in the opposite direction a full 180 degrees away from the first retrieve. If your dog masters this drill, tighten it up to 45 degrees as well.

If at any point throughout the doubles training your dog runs into serious issues staying on track, stop immediately. Take a few steps back and re-work some of the earlier drills. Eventually, your dog will be ready to move on.

PATTERN MEMORY
When your duck dog has aced his drills thus far, it's time to head to the nearest football field. Have your thrower stand on the goal line and back up 25 yards. Your partner should then toss a single retrieve, and you should send your dog. If it goes well, back up

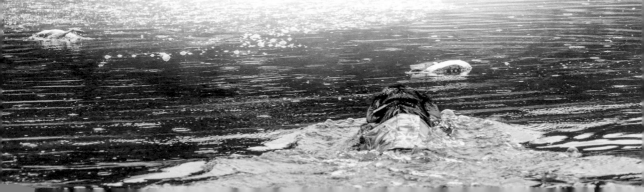

another 25 yards and repeat. Keep this up until your dog is retrieving singles at a full 100 yards.

At this point, return to the 25-yard mark and have the thrower toss the dummy. Once tossed, throw your own dummy as well, and then send your dog. When he brings it to hand, send him for the farther dummy. Again, provided things go well, increase the distance of the memory retrieve (the helper's dummy). Eventually, your dog should be able to retrieve the dummy you toss and then conduct a second memory retrieve up to 100 yards away. This may take five days, or it may take weeks, but it's worth it to build your dog's confidence and help them learn to retrieve on memory.

If you don't have a helper for these drills, you can still conduct the farther retrieve doubles, it just takes longer. Your dog needs to be able to stay or be placed so that you can run out and toss the long retrieve, and then come back to also toss the shorter retrieve.

Conversely, if you have the opportunity to add in a second thrower, by all means do it. This gives you the chance to just control the dog while your two training partners throw the dummies and vary (increase) the length of both retrieves. This changes the dynamics and difficulty of the drill and allows you to monitor simply as the handler.

ADVANCED WORK

If the soccer-field training goes well enough, it's time to start over with the simple 180 drills and work the process again. However, this time will involve new terrain: tall grass, varied locations and then water. I like to pay special attention to the wind when training in tall grass and use wax-based scents on my dummies to encourage the dog to use his nose as well as his eyes.

It's obviously easier to conduct these drills on land than in the water, especially the long-distance doubles, but do your best to find locations that allow you to train as well as possible. Shallow creeks, or hip-wader-friendly ponds are great spots to work on these drills in realistic locations.

As your dog gets more experience working double drills, he'll start to believe that there might be multiple birds to retrieve every time he is sent out. This instills confidence that goes a long ways in the duck boat or blind when two birds do hit the water and your dog is going to be tasked with bringing them both to hand. This is especially important if your dog doesn't actually see both birds go down, which is very common when crouched in the cattails or corn stubble and the melee of an approaching flock and subsequent volley of shots causes a bit of chaos for human and hound alike.

SECTION FOUR
DESTINATIONS

ALASKA PART I: COLD BAY

Benelli soars with the new Super Black Eagle 3.

BY SKIP KNOWLES

THE PROPELLERS THROBBED AS the Penair flight circled and landed on Cold Bay's giant emergency runway, three hours west of Anchorage in the heart of the Aleutian archipelago, one of the harshest places in Alaska.

Sunny and calm, we were jovial upon landing under blue skies, and it was very hard to imagine what would greet us in the morning, just 12 hours later, in this place where

north Pacific storms trade across into the Bering Sea in the waters featured on "Deadliest Catch." It is a raw land of burning cold winds and steaming volcanoes puffing in the distance that at times throw red magma into the night. And the thin jagged peaks of the Rampart Range are like ice fortresses in the distance…

It's a good place for something to be born, or at least born again.

And very soon, it made perfect sense why Benelli had chosen this location to launch the third coming of the legendary Super Black Eagle.

In the pre-dawn, winds were soon gusting to 70 mph, howling straight off the ocean and lashing at our windows, spewing sideways

rain and slush. You could hear storm surf pounding as we awoke at "sunrise," roughly 9:30 a.m. The group of hunters assumed we'd wait for it to calm, that no ducks could fly in that kind of weather.

But that's not the Captain Jeff Wasley way. The lodge door burst open, and Wasley blew in with a gust and stood there, already soaked, with water-drops flecked on his eyeglasses, and murmured "20 minutes and we roll out." Ever more the bearded sea captain than mild-mannered biologist he also is, Wasley started Four Flyways for his great love of ducks and hunting, and he is at the top of the food chain and, well geographically, the world.

Over the next five days we would break an outboard motor far offshore, and stall a jacked-up suburban to the windows in the middle of a gushing river. But the one thing we couldn't break were these guns. Benelli's Super Black Eagle landed just over a

quarter-century ago in 1991 and rose to prominence as the duck man's broadsword through the '90s. The gun set a new standard as one of the first semi-autos to handle 2 ¾", 3" on up to 3.5" shells, when the longer shells were developed to help offset the inferior downrange lethality of steel after lead was banned. Nobody had seen anything quite like the Black Eagle when it came out;

the overall slenderness and the lovely between-the-hands balance, because most the weight is in the receiver where the Inertia-Driven system hides. The shotgun quickly became a waterfowling status symbol and helped a young company that only started building guns in 1967 carve out a niche from a field dominated by centuries-old brands like Browning, Beretta,

Remington and Winchester.

The new SB3 has the same core guts as the original: That simple Inertia-Driven system, built around a powerful compact spring housed within the bolt that is the "engine" for the recoil operating system ("If it ain't broke…" said Benelli Product Manager George Thompson). At least a dozen new design and ergonomic touches elevate the SB3, aimed at lighter weight, better handling and shooter comfort, and above all, less recoil and muzzle rise. It is a super-refined version of the original: softer-kicking, user-friendly, and pure Italian with stylish new accents by Marco Vignaroli on the receiver borrowed from the elegant Ethos model the company recently launched. The accent lines represent the silhouette of a bird in flight, and really pop on the black model without being garish (the gun comes in Mossy Oak Bottomland, Realtree Max-5, matte black and Optifade Timber).

Another critical add for the SB3 also lifted from the Ethos: The "easy locking" détente in the bolt assembly assures the rotating face always seats, even when the gun is bumped on the butt stock or the action is crudded up with residue, a complaint on prior models. Other major tweaks include an improved (third generation) ComforTech stock to redirect recoil with an excellent larger, softer cheek pad for forgiveness.

That's a lot of emphasis on comfort for the tough guys of the outdoors. Nobody is nastier to their guns than waterfowlers. We threw these guns in aluminum boats that pounded through waves, covered them in marine spray, let them bang around in the decoys and get stepped on by muddy dogs streaming saltwater, tossing them on the beach between sessions. And, of course, we shot hundreds of high-velocity, heavy duck loads through them, all in near-freezing conditions. The climate was so harsh, choke tubes were rusted by day two. We were too cold to care.

COLD BAY SURVIVAL

On that first morning of hurricane-force winds, we expected Capt. Jeff to step forward and explain what we would do when the weather died. But you don't work around the weather in Cold Bay, Alaska, you just try to survive it. The Cold Bay experience is one of pristine wilderness, and a bucket-list adventure for trophy species in wild spaces for core waterfowlers. But it's wilderness for a reason. We piled out of the trucks that first dawn, and stood nervously in the gale as we fought to close the doors in the wind, unsure of ourselves in our shiny new Cabela's waders in Max-5, but grateful for all the high-tech Sitka gear clothing. Most of us tromped down to a nearby lake shore—ocean hunting was out of the question with giant surf—and hid not far from the road to hunt. But I had mentioned that I wanted a rare Eurasian teal or wigeon the night prior, and that earned me a death hike. Captain lined a few of us out on a cross-country jaunt in the torrent, dropping off two others at the halfway point. Hoofing around the rugged lakeshore, my guide Mark Vander Zanden often opted to wade over greasy boulders, and I had to use the butt stock of the new gun to catch myself a few times in the slick rocks, submerging it violently past the trigger group like a wading staff.

Three times, wind gusts grabbed the large metal frame pack full of decoys protruding from my back like a sail and nearly drove me into the lake. I quickly learned to walk bent doubled over. It was strange to see winds lift the surface waters off a lake and vaporize them skyward in a reverse rainstorm. The tundra was horribly difficult hiking, like jogging in a ditch full of sponges, until you hit a trail; but here's the problem with that. These nice trails were created by 1,000-pound brown bears, just as heavy-bodied as the famed Kodiak monsters. Lunging over the spongy tundra,

> The tundra was horribly difficult hiking, **like jogging in a ditch full of sponges.**

hitting a trail filled with water but grateful for the hard bottom, I stumbled along a full hour behind Mark and let me tell you, as we strolled past hundreds of half-eaten sockeye and piles of brown bear scat, it was awfully nice to have a reliable 12-gauge with 3.- inch 1⅝-ounce Hevi-Shot loads riding on the carrier in my hand, just in case the Man in the Brown Suit showed up. One stroke of the bolt handle and we would be ready to try to defend ourselves.

We finally struck a tiny bay, hunkered beside a hummock, and threw out a few decoys. The fun started instantly with a pair of stunning drake goldeneyes buzzing through. The first was too fast

but he left his wingman bobbing in the decoys. Matching drake bufflehead appeared next and a clean double on those beauties was followed by some of the biggest mallards on earth splashing feet up. Strangely for the Halloween date, all the birds were already glowing fully-plumed drakes from the far north, and three are headed for the taxidermist. I'd never fired the SB3, and even while wearing arctic-worthy Sitka, this gun was easy to shoot.

Case-in-point. Hiking out, fighting the wind with five heavy ducks bouncing on my strap against my chest and a loaded pack on my back, we somehow heard the rush of wings and turned as a super-sized-mallard burst from the reeds 15 feet below the ledge we trudged along. In a flash I had the gun up, and despite the ducks around my neck, ripped back the bolt handle, turned and crushed that greenhead with one shot at 40 yards. Mallards here are massive, over four pounds, because most do not migrate, and they gorge on salmon eggs and carcasses. Mark was delighted at the shot, though we had to wait a good bit for the wind to bring it ashore.

You can't say much more than that about a shotgun's handling. Or that new oversized bolt handle on the SB3 that I'd needed to chamber a round, or the new grip and trigger design I'd found with soaking thick gloves in a critical split second. The safety has been enlarged as well. The rounded trigger guard is forgiving, and the pistol grip is deeper, allowing both more control and better relationship to access the trigger. A deeper pistol grip reduces recoil by letting you more

into the gun and giving more grip control, eliminating "punch." A deep grip also allows you to use your push-up muscles against recoil too, as your chest is much stronger than just your thumb.

NEXT GEN BLACK EAGLE
The fumbling cold and slippery wet climate was the ideal test for all the accouterments added to the new SBE3, like that redesigned grip and bolt handle, as well as the newly slenderized and enhanced forestock, and especially the new enlarged loading port with big grooves in front of the new trigger guard to smooth feeding. A redesigned carrier/lifter also helps.

It was a grueling five-mile hike, all told, in the unrelenting wind over the squishy thick moss. The gun is long but a pleasure to carry, and lighter than its granddad, the SBE II, right at 7 pounds. I was grateful for the firepower (bears) but also the lack of bulk and heft.

"The engineers handed us the new gun and said they could have made it almost a pound lighter, and wanted to, but I told them no," said, George Thompson, Senior Product Manager with Benelli.

That's really not ideal in a 12-gauge firing waterfowl loads, he said, and he's right. Later, back home on the range, I threw my entire garage stash into the gun, feeding it everything from rusty old Black Cloud to new 3.5" high velocity B&P 1.5-ounce 2s. Buckshot, Hevi-Shot, slugs, 1-ounce dove loads…the gun ate them all, even the cool Hog Wild two-ball loads from Hevi. I only got it to jam once, by firing corroded old shells much

faster than you ever would afield. There was a measured evenness in shot patterns, due to the proven CrioBarrel system. I fired several other quality semi-autos and could detect no difference in recoil versus the gas guns. Pretty cool as a shotgunner to be able to feed a wild mix of loads and shell lengths into a gun and see it spit them all out like a wood chipper. Tungsten, lead, steel, didn't matter. The gun's new two-part elastic carrier latch worked as billed for easier loading to the mag.

At times we would be feeding whatever shells we could grab into the SB3 on the frantic hunts for those stunning saltwater geese, the Pacific black brant, the absolute highlight of the Cold Bay trip. Brant from three flyways converge on the giant Izembek Lagoon to gorge on eel grass before migration, the highest concentration of the birds in the world. Jumping in the layout boats 20 feet apart in the wind and waves, Jeff Puckett and I were barely settled in when gobs of the geese came in low and straight. I doubled right away, and with only one bird left for a limit, laid the Benelli down and focused on calling for Jeff, who quickly caught up. A single came high and right, then centered up the middle as I called. He was right in my wheelhouse but I waited to see if he turned right, in which case I would nail him. Left, and he's Jeff's. At 20 he lifted left and I yelled "shoot him Jeff!" into the wind. Jeff popped up and missed, then cracked him hard. The retrieve boat yelled out "double-banded" when picking the bird up and we shout with joy, as Jeff scored the bird hunting trophy of a lifetime. For three days, the brant hunting held just as strong, with so much action we rotated through the layout boats and even the guides took turns. We started calling ourselves the Hecklers, because there was always a half-dozen guys on the beach, watching the layouts just offshore, helping call in birds and cheering the shooters' hits and especially their misses.

It was like a surreal dream come true for brant fanatics. Each day I'd bang out two birds within five minutes, then calm down, enjoy the hunt, and wait on a third. The fact that everyone pounded out

limits of these saltwater geese and nobody had trouble using an unfamiliar gun says an awful lot about the design. It was a pure Alaska experience—eagles kept stealing our birds—despite the lack of local crab legs from these famous waters. The brant made up for it. When Wasley grilled those breasts, we all wondered how it was that brant were not extinct. On par with elk tenderloin, nothing like any waterfowl we'd eaten.

Brant die easy, but not sea ducks. Chasing them the last day, we were running the heaviest Hevi-Shot loads available, trying to kill the biggest duck in North America, the ghostlike Pacific eider. It was tough hunting, and few came close to limits but we all took home birds for the wall. On the bigger water in the bouncing layouts, these zipping sea ducks were some of the hardest birds to hit, the water rough enough I missed twice trying to finish off a cripple and laughed aloud—I'd missed a sitting duck! Humbling, after making hero shots from Canada to Louisiana

all season. I made up for it by doubling on drake harlequin, one of the prettiest birds on earth, managing to miss the hen flying between them.

Freezing saltwater aside, a layout boat is a perfect gun test because it is a lousy place to shoot from. Essentially a super-low kayak, you can't shoot far to the right or left nor easily straight up, and the whole thing is moving in the waves.

The guns had a few mild hiccups in Alaska's extreme conditions, due to the fact we were shooting prototypes and the difficulty of finding a consistent shoulder mount in bobbing layout boats, I'm certain. Lighter than its predecessor, the SBE3 should kick harder but the test group of hunters agreed it was the softest-kicking Super Black Eagle ever, by far, and that the trademark system of rubber chevrons in the redesigned third generation ComforTech stock seem to reduce muzzle lift and combine with the super-soft, oversized cheek piece (which houses its own flexible shim) to soften the feel of shooting.

That cheek piece feels odd to touch, so big and soft like the tundra, but is the most noticeable and effective recoil reducing aspect, as the gun simply can't punch you in the face anymore if you pull up a hasty mount and lack a good cheek weld. That is normally where you pay.

The Black Eagle series was already a wingshooter's dream and absolutely the last hunting shotgun you'll ever need. This gun assures that legacy will prosper.

In a flash I had the gun up, and despite the ducks around my neck, **ripped back the bolt handle and crushed the greenhead at 40 yards.**

The OTHER Down Under

Bagging exotic ducks and bonding with buddies... it doesn't get better than Argentina

BY SKIP KNOWLES

THE TV CAMERA GUYS WERE pouting, and MOJO mogul Terry Denmon was growing frustrated. Once again, at the urging of outfitter Diego Munoz, my old friend, the entire party had limited with way too many ducks before the light was very good for TV work. Smoking gun barrels showed we were pretty much all guilty, Denmon included.

"We gotta get one thing straight," Denmon started, making it clear this could not keep happening because he'd come to film MOJO Outdoors. But it did happen, again and again, to just to a slightly less degree. A little different from the normal TV experience where you pray for enough action to can a show. We kept blowing it because we'd all been to Argentina and had good shooting before, but this year was different. The hunting was ridiculous.

Finishing fast pleases Munoz, as he doesn't like to burn his duck holes. We were hunting a couple hours north of Diego's base camp in Las Flores where he outfits with is lovely wife Cody. There was simply a lot more water to the north this year. That's what makes Diego such a top duck killer—he will go where the ducks are; most outfitters here will not. And despite the shift in locale we were still just a few hours' drive from Buenos Aires, in the same grassy flat farmlands and marsh country that teems with ducks.

A lot of water had come to northern Argentina, and Diego lives for that. Three years prior, we had been flyfishing Patagonia when

dire reports came in that the north was flooding and people in Buenos Aires were suffering. You would have thought Diego had won the lottery, he was so happy. This year, he had been torturing us for months with reports of the lights-out duck hunting. Now it was late July, and finally it was our turn.

Gone were the comfortable blinds at the edge of the water of past

years; all submerged. We stood in a deep cold marsh in the reeds, ammo pouches underwater. A large American fellow took a swim after stumbling. It was tough wading and Denmon's strange-looking new wading staff proved as brilliant as his magnetic Pick Stick was for picking up empty shells on these volume shoots.

Without a staff, you were just one nutria hole away from a dunking, but all that is forgotten the second a gun goes off. Mild weather, mobs of birds and epic food and camaraderie…it's a heady mix when you are with guys who know how to keep it fun. It's hard to get in a bad mood, impossible to stay in one.

"Why you do that?" Diego shouted, after we had agreed to stop shooting. He was talking to the ducks still dropping in and hovering right over us. "WHY you do dat!" he shouted, grabbing my gun, stuffing shells in it and blasting away. The suave green-eyed Argentine is a phenomenal shot, fast and liquid smooth. He is a larger-than-life character, crass but funny, a man who speaks five languages and was halfway through med school when he snapped and went hunting for the rest of his life, starting Las Flores wingshooting and lining up with Ramsey Russell, that globe-trotting waterfowl travel broker.

Diego commented constantly on my shooting. "Nice shot, ass-munch!" he'd say when I clobbered a bird. He says the exact same thing every time I miss, but with sarcasm.

The non-stop banter between Denmon and Ramsey is a gut-buster, for two sharper-tongued rednecks never lived. And Diego, even though an outfitter, is an honorary South American redneck. Like when he tries to get me to shoot some fierce-looking predatory bird stalking our spread.

"Keel dat bird, Skipper, they eat my baby ducks," he'd say, pointing.

"No way man, I don't know what's legal," I'd say.

"Ah, come on, Munch, shoot it, keel dat mother…"

Terry cackled at this exchange and made fun of Diego the rest of the trip, a running joke, faking his accent but sounding more Mexican than Argentine, with an odd Mississippi flair. "Ah come on, Skeeper, keel dat bird, choot dat mudder," Denmon would say, pointing to some harmless songbird. "They eat the baby grasshoppers, I love my baby grasshoppers…"

Unlike most hunts down here where you are just starting your journey by getting to BA, with Diego you will decompress from a 14-hour flight the same day you arrive, just like we did: Wade out into a reedy small wetland, deploy a couple dozen decoys, kick back and slowly work into the rhythm of smacking teal and pintails that are humping it with a strong tailwind, screaming over-the-shoulder-shots at birds going so fast they would carry far from where you shot them. I had a blind to myself, nice because no rush to shoot. A few birds buzzed so fast I didn't even get my gun up, and got burned a lot. A few rosey-billed pochards showed, the big black corn-eating duck with the hump nose that is the prized target down here, but mostly the seven species of exotic teal showed along with two types of pintails. The soft white Argentine winter light bathed us, a perfect launch to the trip.

Next morning, the excitement thrummed in our stomachs as thousands of ducks flushed in the headlights of the truck before we threw out decoys, birds like giant bats coming at us in the dark. Denmon was grinning ear to ear. When the shooting started at dawn it was roseys right, left, almost too much. Which is why we got in trouble with the camera guys.

Me and Ramsey defended the left, while Denmon and his girlfriend Annette Manpier took down birds from the right, Diego running commentary non-stop, prodding everyone to shoot, shoot, shoot…

Denmon still prefers U.S.-style duck hunting over South America, but loves to come here for the overall experience, like getting to hunt wild pigeons over decoys, which he loves. I asked him why he preferred Louisiana duck hunting over the amazing shooting here.

"They don't tend to get as big flocks down here," he said, "and there's nothing more exciting than a big flock of greenheads. And the ducks here don't decoy real well and they don't call good, either."

That is true: Guides in Argentina mostly whistle at the ducks. Mojos are simply murderous here, as lethal as when they very first appeared in the U.S. It's a different experience, Denmon continued, in that the hunt camps emphasize good food and wine, and relaxation. It's a bit like travelling back in time to an older, less-industrialized American landscape.

"A lot of it reminds me of the rural south where I grew up, and I like that. Their farming methods are behind North America's. Down here you see the gauchos (cowboys on actual horses) all over the place, and they still do more things with people than machines."

Howard Whybrew of Cupped Up Outdoors, maker of the Muskrat Hut, was in camp, and slaying ducks over both water and land. His cameraman Jeff Berg, an accomplished 'fowler from Washington state, noted that the roseys were a real challenge to shoot. "For a big duck they really turn and burn like no mallard." Berg, who had never been to Argentina, was overwhelmed the first morning when dozens of ducks were downed in no time. Berg is the kind of guy you love to meet on these trips. Another American in camp explained why he does not see hunting Argentina as elitist, just smart. Leon Ghetti, of Byram, Mississippi, owner of Dump Trucks, Inc., takes time away from running 50 trucks to hunt here each year.

"I worked for 50 years without a vacation and ended up on a hunt down here by asking someone if I could come with them. I thought I needed an invitation or something. Since then I've been six times. Also Uruguay and Nicaragua, but nothing compares to a hunt with Diego. The reason is, he participates. He eats with us, goes out in the field and hunts and calls the ducks… he's a hands-on operator, a working guide who does his best to make it the best hunt you can have. I have already planned three seven-day trips for next year."

"And Diego will go find the ducks," he continued. "Other guides have one spot and if it's a bad water year there, well that's it. I met guys on the plane on the way here that said where they'd planned to go it was flooded out so the outfitter told them they'd have to go to Cordoba and go dove hunting. To a duck hunter, that ain't right.

"The expense is relative. It's cheap compared to the duck club racket," said Ghetti. "Back home the only clubs that kill any amount of ducks you have to spend a quarter-million dollars to join. On the river near me they've bought up 4,000 acres, created a club, built 40-acre ponds and have a full-time attendant, and just the dues alone will pay for a seven-day trip to Argentina where you will kill more ducks in seven days than in 10 years in the U.S., with no standing in the freezing water with ice all over you. It's a no-brainer. This is wingshooter's paradise. "

Ramsey books for Diego, but it's where he hunts, too. "Diego's deal is volume and shooting ducks. There are fancier lodges, but with Diego you are going to shoot your birds."

Everyone in our camp thought the food was plenty fancy. You will eat enough duck here to assuage your conscience. Roseybills prepared by cute little Rosy, camp chef, are marinated in an herb and egg batter, dredged in crumbs and fried Milanesa style. Deadly. With a glass of Malbec, we constantly wrecked our appetite before the main courses of famed Argentina beef (regarded as the best in the world) and steady plates of Argentine enchiladas, empanadas, more ducks, red deer...it's a culinary cultural immersion.

And the hunting is like compacting a few seasons in the states into a few days. A retriever could never keep up here. You shoot unplugged guns, yet only load two shells at a time because you will burn through your ammo too fast. And when the roseys are thick, these big ducks push all the pretty smaller birds like ringed teal and white-cheeked pintail out of the area. It's a place a duck man needs to go once just to see the incredible species.

"Brazilians!" yelled Diego and I swung and dropped a teal that honestly gave me chills when the flock banked in the sun. The entire back of the Brazilian teal's wings shone metallic blue-green, not just the speculum.

On one evening field set on the edge of a muddy corn pond, loads of ducks came toward us but rose too high at the last minute because of a powerline in front of us. Still, we knocked down five dozen Roseybills and pintails, and saw some stunner white-cheeked pintails, one of the

more beautiful ducks on the planet, along with a pile of whistlers.

Next day, Ramsey and I were having a slow hunt tucked in a big reed patch, with no wind, when suddenly the sky lit up and so did the shooting. Rainstorms were dropping buckets on us. I admired the old battle axe gutting it out in his ratty wax cloth jacket that I wouldn't let my dog sleep on, hunkered under an equally old Jones cap, his belt-bandolier of shells ensuring his demise if he fell in. With no hood, it rained right down

his neck. I was warm and dry in a fancy new BANDED jacket.

"I'm fine, shoot, don't worry, this ain't nothing," he said when he saw my concern.

The mornings were always a mad shootzen-fest, but evenings could be like stateside hunting. Birds zipping in right and left, promising to finish, only to flare, hook the wind and blow out. The next morning with Denmon, we waded into duck weed just under our armpits, in deep, cold water. We saw no birds at all. Trust your guide. It came on like a

switch. Ducks hovered all around the Mojo like moths at a flame.

Early in the trip, I had not shot the greatest, so Diego took us for an evening pigeon shoot, a trick that always makes his hunters improve. Difficult shots in the trees on high-flying birds, and I shot a few dozen squab. The next day I could not miss ducks. We all have those days when we couldn't hit water if we fell out of a boat, but the inverse is true, too. Down here, you can really hit your groove. I was snap-shooting the afterburner zipping-past birds like a nervous twitch, tripling a few times, and somehow sucking to earth a pair of whistlers so high they should have been "seats locked and in the upright position." You forget how lethal a shotgun can be.

It never gets old. Just as the hunts start to feel routine, tree ducks show up, or white-faced whistlers, or gorgeous chiló wigeon, or silver teal…

Denmon shot so well I started calling him Terry Demon. Like he says, the shooting is cool, but it's the broader experience. I went for a mid-day jog, trying to run away from all that food, and passed a gushing stream. Young and old people were hauling out catfish and some kind of bass. Hiking up a country lane, I wondered why this entire country is more crammed with birds than back home. Brown upland rockets, perdiz, feed all over the roadside while giant pigeons flock in the trees, amid huge nests of gorgeous green parakeets bursting from every other eucalyptus tree. Giant, heavy, raptor-looking birds called "screamers" glare from the fields. And, of course, las palomas— doves, doves, doves.

Seeing these strange things is why travel is renewing. Like

a random pile of small snakes still wiggling in the road. Diego theorized that a huge bird of prey had eaten too many and puked them up. Then there was the injured green parakeet that became Diego's buddy, sitting on his shoulder in the marsh.

One memorable shoot was the slowest, a morning hunt in tall reeds in too-deep water, due to 12 more inches of rain flooding the country just prior to our visit, blowing out roads and railways. Pintail and teal swerved in left, and we lost them in the sun. We were too close to Ramsey and Leon, but it became a good time, more like a dove hunt, as we yelled back and forth. Ducks crumpled as they flew over our friend's blind, then a few seconds later you hear the shots.

I challenged Diego to a triple, but just then two long skinny ducks flashed in the sun and headed our way . . . the elegant white-cheeked pintails. We waited on more Roseys, and Diego about made good on the triple, but I

snaked the last bird out from under him. "You got right, I got left,' I said, down to my last shell as they came in straight but high. I swung through from the rear until the bird disappeared, just like daddy taught me. Diego fired in unison, two ducks splashing behind us. It had taken us a few hours to get our share, but hunting with an old buddy was as good as it gets, and at times we'd wrecked flocks of Roseys like Texans banging teal.

Our final morning shoot was one big fluid memory that slowed time. We started being more selective as our collective consciousness told us a grand moment was unfolding, one of those you live for. We started letting all the overhead zingers have a pass along with the backside swingers because far more than we could ever shoot were doing it right; low and straight in.

That is why you suffer through that 14-hour flight. The only bad thing about hunting Argentina? Well, the shooting does get a little too hot for TV cameras at times.

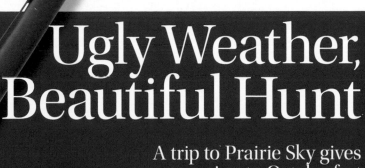

Ugly Weather, Beautiful Hunt

A trip to Prairie Sky gives new meaning to Octoberfest

IMAGES AND WORDS BY SKIP KNOWLES

THE BIRDS CAME IN LIKE A WATERFOWLING CLICHÉ, HOT ON THE tail of severe weather. Dark black in the low light, the ringnecks appeared low and tight in fighter formation, pumping straight forward through the freezing wind. Squads of wigeon lofting higher showed in the heavy grey sky and sucked right into the spread, rarely looking twice. Fast and sleek, small groups of gadwall followed the shoreline at mid-elevation in a faster, circling pattern, always looking twice.

Tough hunting under blue early October skies had given way to the kind of day you live for as soon as the weather had gone to hell. It's a common theme in the pothole country surrounding the 2,000 acres of South Dakota heaven known as Prairie Sky Ranch: Fair weather turns foul and the fowling turns fair, in this case, just in time for our last day.

The pothole country is best seen from the sky, where it looks as though a giant prehistoric soaking wet Lab descended from heaven and shook off, and everywhere a droplet landed a pond ringed with cattails formed permanently. Of course we all know there is nothing permanent about potholes in today's world, and the view inspires you to protect what we have left. A humdinger of a morning hunt over great dogs doesn't hurt, either.

The hunt was sponsored by Sport-DOG, and for someone who loves to see retrievers in action, the trip was a three-day action clinic of both guides and SportDOG staff, who are really rather hard to tell apart, since core hunting values and dog ownership are at the center of their company culture. Clay Thompson, who manages the training category of products, lives out here on the prairie near Aberdeen, chasing birds all over the country, and says the company creed "Gear the way you'd design it" could just as easily say "we live this." Most of the dogs in brochures and ads belong to employees, who are almost all core dog owners and hunters. Their active field input is combined with that from pro staff members like Tom Dokken, and the results are much more user-friendly tools for both gun dogs and the people they own.

Still, gear and gadgets are terrific, but they're a lot better if you can see it work in extreme conditions.

For the first few days, temps were in the 60s, and a west wind each morning had us staring straight into the glaring early fall sun, tears welling in our eyes as we tried to follow birds. The first morning, four ducks came suddenly from nowhere, cupping down into the little pond right as they reached where the sun glared at us on the water. As we've all done many times, my barrel caught up with a big drake just as it disappeared into the searing white ball of light and I squeezed the trigger. I expected the crushed bird to spill from the sun stream down to the water with a splash. Not this time. One shot, no duck, and I was left with a burned out blue-white hot spot in my vision every time I blinked, wondering where that bird had gone.

Soon after, a mature full plume greenhead joined a colored up sprig on my straps in an early-season shocker, and I was grateful to get

two fully-feathered big ducks so early. But overall, it was tough, as we hunted 'til noon just to scratch a couple ducks apiece. The next morning the wind shifted after

Echo is **so cross-eyed,** the black Lab takes a hand mark looking off the wrong direction, with one eye fishing and the other cutting bait, yet she lines out and hunts like a dream.

dawn and we were off the X, and moved into deep grass at the far end of a pond. We shot solid half-limits, cheering one lucky duck, a big greenhead everyone missed at 40 yards that flew away terrified.

One of the best retrieves—and retrievers—I was to see all season happened soon after, when we sailed a dead-in-flight drake up on a grassy hillside a full 300 yards away. Head guide Stephen Rosasco steered Echo, his cross-eyed wonder dog, straight up on the hill, whistled for a "sit," then with one hand gesture put Echo right on the bird. Just awesome. Echo is so cross-eyed, the black Lab takes a hand mark looking off the wrong direction, with one eye fishing and the other cutting bait, she lines out and hunts like a dream.

A CHANGE IN THE WEATHER
The prairie taketh away, but the prairie giveth, too, when the weather turns. That night we cringed when a brutal cold front struck hard and fast, with temps in the teens, gusts to 45 mph and sustained winds in the 30s, putting wind chill God-knows-how-low. Sideways sleet and rain was so bad that in the pre-dawn

we joked we'd be ready to quit by the time the last decoy was put out.

"We're either going to murder them today or it's going to be awful," I said to my cabin roommate Darrel Douglas of SportDOG.

He agreed. "Some days with wind like this they just raft up on big water, some days they fly for you," he said.

Foregoing a proper blind, we buried ourselves deep in cattails like new fawns and surprisingly, it took the edge off the weather. It was a dreary scene, until grey daylight slowly appeared and the ducks never quit.

After two slow days, I banged away and my limit, mostly ringnecks, was done in 28 minutes, including dog work! I could have slowed down. SportDOG engineer Chris Morgan and Darrell took their time, let the birds circle and leave, enjoying the work of Darrell's big strong black Lab Oz, and we had six species in the bag by 11. Everyone forgot the cold; especially when Morgan dropped a big redhead drake.

With my gun stowed, I got to really soak in the dog action. The dauntless Oz did good work in miserable wind that made it tough to smell birds, a gale so strong it put a five-inch chop on the little pond. Under such conditions, the need for long–distance phone calls between dog and hunter is apparent. The Dokken-trained Oz needed little help, but it was good to see that gone are the old days of whistle your dog, yell at your dog, then shock your dog if he ignores you. Now, you can send a friendly reminder in the form of either a vibration the dog associates with the collar and a pending electric "nick," or the nick itself, which can be toned down so low it is barely detectable; more a reminder than a truly negative reinforcement.

SportDOG products are so much more accessible price-wise than good e-collars were when I had my best retriever back in the '90s. Entry-level price points are lower and product features are so superior it's like comparing old Damascus steel flintlock doubles to a Beretta Silver Pigeon. Darrell was running the WetlandHunter SD-425, a compact, weatherproof e-coller for the waterfowler, and after dozens of icy retrieves, the little unit held up under brutal conditions.

Dogs aren't wholly weatherproof, either. Warm temps like we saw on the first part of our hunt create obvious hardships, but when the cold weather descends it brings a new set of hydration challenges and calorie demands. SportDOG treats dogs like athletes, and their line of C9 canine supplements and electrolyte energy and hydration products for dogs are unprecedented.

Gadgets are great, but seeing them work reliably in the battery-killing elements best for waterfowling gave me a lot of confidence in this new wave of electronic training tools.

SportDOG's Gretchen Goodson collects a pheasant dinner.

IF YOU GO

Prairie Sky Guest & Game Ranch is located in northeast South Dakota, surrounded by wetlands, native prairie, turkeys, deer, bison and loads of other native wildlife. Proprietor Bruce Prin is a lanky tall old cowboy with an aw-shucks demeanor that is so pleasant you want to haul him out to the duck blind with you. Besides fishing, riding, and the famous duck and goose hunting, a big part of the Prairie Sky experience is enjoying seeing your friends miss "tame" pheasants, and miss them a lot. A few of the gun writers on our trip derided pen-released pheasant hunting as unchallenging or somehow beneath them, which made watching them whiff deeply gratifying. The dogs did catch a few birds in the high wind when noise concealed our approach—but many times I saw guys running out of ammunition long before the hunting was over because the same wind made birds a real challenge to hit. I make no apologies; I love shooting any pheasant. Pen-raised or not, they are so good eating! Hiking across the golden hills, we tested the UplandHunter SD-1875 e-collar/beeper combo on a host of pointers, and the GPS-based TEK system proved invaluable when dogs locked on point in heavy cover, standing corn or deep cattails. A real lifesaver for the upland hunter. The Ranch has lovely spacious cabins surrounding wetlands a short walk from the main lodge.

For more information on Prairie Sky visit www.prairieskyranch.com.

MEXICAN
revolution

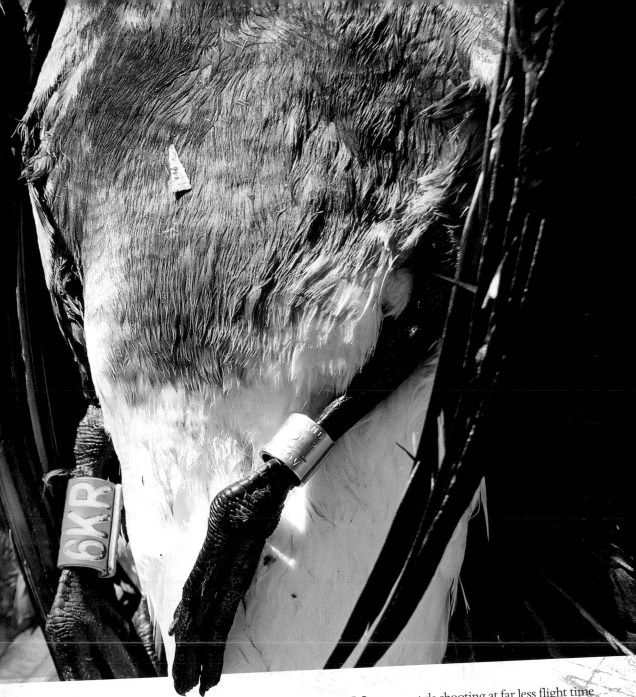

The original North American wingshooting dream destination is back

BY SKIP KNOWLES

WHILE NOT A TOTAL MEXI-CAN standoff, Americans at least have been stand-offish about heading south of the border to enjoy what was for decades prior North America's great fair-weather wing-shooting escape.

And that's too bad. Mexico has everything going for it. Argentina-style shooting at far less flight time and expense, and the weather we all dream of escaping to at the same time our sordid, soul-sucking late winter is lingering in the States (whereas in Argentina, winter duck hunting occurs in our summer).

But the murderous border wars between drug lords created too much fear over the past decade or so, and Gringo traffic to pursue the great numbers of deer, dove, and waterfowl slowed to a crawl, along with the famous bass and deep-sea fishing. Travel bureaus claimed the major tourist cities safe, but not the backcountry, and even so, reports would filter down about a kidnapping in Cancun or a shootout in Mazatlan.

So I'd sure been hesitant to sign on for a trip to Mexico, and these things weighed on me, but my lust for a black brant hunt got the better of me. Despite hunting all over the continents, I hadn't even seen a brant in years, and the idea of hunting Pacific black brant right on the Sea of Cortés across from Baja in late winter was more than I could stand. I had to go. Booking agent Ramsey Russell assured me if you were not looking for trouble or trying to relive The Hangover and stuck to the areas you were supposed to go with the people you were supposed to be there with, there would be no unwanted trouble.

Now it was late February, I was on my way, and my flight was

canceled due to yet another Illinois blizzard in the never-ending polar vortex. Worse, Ramsey was starting in with the shoulda-been-here-yesterday stories on the phone, padding my expectations after a year of hype. He cited clouds of ducks, and eight banded brant falling in just one shoot the week prior to my arrival...prior. But now the weather had turned, he reported, and it had grown unseasonably hot in Hermasillo and Obregon in the state of Sonora, and I was already rolling my eyes. Blaming a heat wave? If heat hurts your hunt in Mexico you have a problem. Stuck in the Illinois blizzard, the idea of a sub-tropical heat wave only made a frozen drink sound better.

I re-booked a flight for the next day, and that was the end of all stress for the next week. The flight from Dallas into Hermasillo was casual and low-key, and getting my shotgun through customs was no big deal. Nobody asked for bribes, and from start to finish I never felt uncomfortable or met a menacing glare.

Big, gregarious, Frank Ruiz has outfitted out of Obregon for decades.

A half-dozen American hunters were already in camp when we arrived, greeted by Frank with cold drinks from his sharp-dressed staff. Inside, the place is a hunter's palace, a veritable natural history museum of birds and animal heads,

I even found my safety. A fully-plumed, later-than-late season drake cinnamon teal came to hand, my first ever, and my first bird in Mexico, ever.

A dawn flurry gave way to an hour of quiet, and with eight or so ducks down it was a nice start for me and Ramsey, but not the kind of hunt for which Mexico is known. The winds shifted slightly, and once it turned on the action was dirty-good. Soon, I was digging for more shells in my bucket seat and I hear Ramsey say, "OK, OK, some from the left now… more still coming from straight out, straight out. Three more. Oh, here's more from the right…and some from behind…"

Bewildered now at trying to mentally track the action, I looked up to see he pretty much had been spot on: We had different groups working on every side and still more circling.

Glorious late winter shovelers in full tuxedo mode were stunning in the Sonoran sun, only outshined by bands of pintail with long quills flowing off their backsides. Teal of three types were a constant challenge, and we had chances at a gorgeous trophy subspecies—Mexican mallards. Rounding things out were a few other favorites of mine in the loveliest plumage I had ever witnessed them, gorgeous gaddies with white blazes and auburn accents, and the odd bluebill zipping through the mix, always in a hurry. Thirty-something ducks fell to our shots; an epic day without seeming like overdoing it. Back at the ramp, we saw other groups shot far more birds, but well within the law. Regional allocations are awarded to guides to act as their

all magnificent specimens, the result of Frank's globetrotting outdoor enthusiasm.

DUCK HUNTING, BUT WARMER

At dawn, the airboats lined out in the humid darkness, humming toward a tidal marsh of vast deep grasses that looked like the Everglades as we twisted our way through trails and over bushy obstacles. The marsh here is green and breathes saltwater in on the flood tide and exhales water so fresh on the ebb tide that cows appear from cover and drink from it.

Wings slit the air. A flicker of motion from the right sped into the dekes and I reflexively slap-shot the teal without thinking. Which was good, because if I'd known exactly what it was I'd have probably frozen up and missed, if

limits, and in this case it was the last week, so if your outfitter has not "tagged out" so to speak, if you are in the last groups, you can make it rain.

Light jackets in the mornings and we were down to shorts by 8 a.m. I thought of the blizzard back home and it was hard to believe. I was so giddy over the cinnamon teal I couldn't stop grinning. The only thing I wanted worse was a brant.

Back at "camp," we were soon chomping on the kind of hors d'oeuvres that make it really tough to not over-do it before the authentic barbacoa chicken and steaks came, and I began a true daytime appreciation tour of the lodge. The service at Gabino's was the best I've ever had in the hunting world, with a cold drink always waiting when you arrive back at the lodge, the guys whisking your gear away

style of flight. They would probably flare like eiders or long-tails too, skirting an obvious blind at 40 yards, never to turn back.

And that would be fine. I'm an ocean freak anyway and would be happy if I could scratch one down

ward then lifting up hundreds of feet in the air, very light in their motion, not heavy and steady at all. Then here they come again, before whirring in another direction to make you panic, before settling out and zooming straight in and finishing right in your lap, feet-down right smack in the dekes.

The two of us flagged with our hats and grunted like divers with our mallard calls, as with each approach they slowly faked left and right. Somehow they whirl and spin, despite having a relatively large body (about like a snow goose) connected to rather diminutive, pointy, wings that would appear to lack the surface area needed to make them fly so effortlessly.

The first group of 10 or so came in and veered, and we let them go at 35 yards. I was sick. What if that was our only shot? Anxious, Ramsey ran out and made a hole in the middle of our large blob of brant decoys, while I yammered at the guides in my terrible Spanish to leave the spread alone as they

> The winds shifted slightly, and once it turned on
> **the action was dirty-good.**

and your guns appearing the next day sparkling clean inside and out. I found an extreme cold threat actually did exist in Sonora—if you drank a frozen beverage too fast you'd get a nasty headache.

BLACK MAGIC

I could see it all in my head. The brant would come in low on the deck and in small numbers, pounding heavily across the water with straight steady wingbeats like big black eiders, I imagined, in that heavy one-dimensional sea duck

and smell and hear the sea, and just seeing fish jumping all around the boat as we motored to the blind made me happy.

Imagine my waterfowler's delight when I saw I was dead wrong. Brant are in fact these magic birds that came in sneakily off the open sea to our stand-up blind on the sand bars at the back of a huge bay, and often in flocks of dozens. Dancing in over the dunes from over a mile away, they appear to have a visible joy in their flight as they loft about, swooping down-

boated over to repair the hole we created in the blob. Seriously. Twice.

The hole worked like magic. The next two birds snuck right in on us while we chatted. I called left bird, and they crossed right at the finish as we shot. Both dropped at the shots and I swatted the left side bird as it tried to keep going. The right bird proved to be double-banded, and I couldn't argue with Ramzilla because cameras were rolling (for World of Beretta). Besides, the guy with the dog wins that argument, anyway. Ramsey added two more to his long string of bands from the week before, and that was the only banded brant any guy in camp saw of the dozens shot on my trip. You can get into bands big-time with brant, but it's always hit or miss. But that was another wild thing about this trip: Ramsey's dog. I did not expect to come and hunt over an awesome retriever from the States, but his killer yellow Lab Cooper made the flight. "Just paperwork, man, preparation. No big deal," he said.

Pelicans sometimes made us eager with their size at great distance, but then you'd see the flap-flap-glide, flap-flap-gli-i-i-i-ide and know they weren't brant. We had some brant flare and not come, but action was steady and just the two of us cut into a pile of the black geese. We quit around a dozen birds when I called it, because to me they are such a cool species, I felt like I'd just shot a dozen deer, and was unsure of total populations. I later learned there are upwards of 150,000 in the Pacific flyway, and they are widely considered under-counted in the aerial counts at Izembek Lagoon in Alaska, where most stop on the migration to gorge on eel grass. The minuscule number of hunters that visit Mexico surely have minuscule impact.

Always a fan of the pintail over the garish wood duck, I found the handsome brant, in all his dark mystery, with that lovely white collar and chestnut brown against black and white, to be the absolute embodiment of understated elegance. Combined with the love of the ocean so many of us have, they are a profoundly beautiful and evocative bird...as well as fabulous eating.

What I can say about Mexico is that I simply can't wait to go back, and that I deeply enjoyed this relaxing trip. Escaping the bitter northern winter to bag bucket-list birds under warm skies in late February was purely sublime. On day three, taking a break from waterfowl to shoot a hundred gorgeous white-wing doves in an hour was none too shabby, either, though the 40-plus yard shots humbled my wingshooting.

That first cinnamon teal was like a ghost from a fantasy, and those undulating lines of brant working inward toward our dekes are seared in my brain forever, locked in with all the good stuff nobody can ever take away from you.

Ledges, Labs and Lobsta!

Two days on a Maine eider hunt is a sensory-saturating experience

BY SKIP KNOWLES

ON A TRIP TO MAINE TO HUNT North America's biggest duck, I was determined to write about the whole Maine coastal experience, not just the birds and the shooting.

There's so much more to it than just the hunting, and it was all there waiting for us. Stonington is a stunning seaside setting, like being trapped in a postcard, the people friendly and warm, the views and sunsets just lovely and the food is the best. Linda Powell of Mossberg made sure of that. She was leading this adventure to have editors test the new Flex pump as well as recoil reduction systems; one of the world's toughest shotguns on the world's toughest sea ducks.

We would not be roughing it except when out on the freezing sea. Life ashore would be laid back, walking the charming wharfs and shops full of books and old decoys, and eating scallops that were on the ocean floor earlier that morning. I couldn't wait to capture it all.

But soon as we were out hunting, I knew I would skip over most of that stuff. It is window dressing, to an avid fowler. Lovely indeed, but window dressing. The most

enthralling part of it all is still the hunt, and why a duck man simply has to do an open-water hunt out on the reefs of Penobscot Bay. Because this is what it's like…

Sitting in the dark on a rock ledge where men before us have done so for centuries, we watch the day creep its way to life from far off distances across the ocean, spreading long fingers of light over the water to the sound of small waves gushing around the rocks at our feet. The subtle splashing noises of birds draws your eyes, and they can be seen stirring from the waters and slowly to flight as though rising from within the sea itself, not off its surface. Lobster boats with green and white lights purposefully splice through the oily calm, pushing still more birds to flight and forcing a deep bass diesel rumble over the water, where sound is amplified and carried.

The sights and sounds engulf you because on this rock ledge far offshore you are part of it, just as much as the curious harbor seal that is slipping around in the decoys with his slick gray head and huge black eyes looking straight at you. You wonder what he is thinking. You also wonder what the sea duck men who brought you here are thinking.

"With the scallop draggin' I'll be surprised if we don't get some birds moving around," says Brad Allen, the eider man.

The calm is sheared with instant tension and a secret dread in your stomach when one of the old boys behind you says forcefully "Out front! Don't move!" The tension mounts as these impossibly big, striking, white-and-black ducks, moving so much faster than they appear to be, pump their wings toward you and toward the moment of truth…

You decide when and try to breath, swing through past the yellow bill, and fire, the dull pop of the gun muted by the ocean's vastness, strangely quieter than a normal shot. Birds tumble, and one needs more shooting. The dog launches into the cold green water, also shrunken by the vastness of the sea, cutting a small V thru the waves more like a big muskrat than the boisterous beast that stomped your thighs in the boat earlier, nearly knocking you off the gunwales.

With humility and awe you behold an enormous heavy eider in hand, so striking and huge and solid-feeling, like an emperor penguin with wings. Looking out at the sun-lit horizon where the waves fade into the mirror-slick of mercurial mirage, white flare-ups and flashes are seen at a great distance. These are splashes from seabirds that somehow erupt like mini white geysers where they are landing a full mile away, an optical miracle of the sea, and the day has just started and this will go on for hours, sure as the tide is rising to fill the rocky cracks, forcing your steady retreat.

This is what it is all about, and why it's worth it. Because at first, it's easy to think, "Whoever thought hunting the North Atlantic in December is a good idea…" It is cold, yes, but bearable, if you miss the storms. A flashback: I remember sitting on the reef next to Powell and watching my steady spitting of sunflower seeds form a glossy glassy stalagmite, freezing in the cold breeze as fast as I expectorated.

Yet a core cadre of committed hunters cannot get enough. Though technically a do-it-yourself, public lands hunt, we would be lost with-

out the Ducks Unlimited guys who hosted us.

"This is a great group of guys, deeply passionate about sea duck hunting," Powell says of the men she has hunted with for seven years. None are actual guides, but cigar-chomping hunt leader and DU

regional director Bill Brown has formidable knowledge of sea-ducking, and Brad Allen is the state biologist with a singular obsession for ciders. Dr. Grant Brees, a retired veterinarian, and Wally Martin round out the group that braved the slippery solid granite boat ramp in the pre-dawn.

I remember sitting on the reef, watching my steady spitting of **sunflower seeds** form a glassy frozen stalagmite.

That first day was unforgettable. Scoter, the intrepid Lab owned by Brees, scored an amazing double retrieve. A hen and then a giant drake fell to my shots, but as if to prove it was not due to skill, I next tried to fire with an empty chamber, jerking the pump's forestock violently to recover and bang a drake, which took off swimming. I joked as the boat chased the bird; "they're doing all the work, if it's banded, do they get it or do I?" I was kidding, but they weren't when the radio crackled "Hey, who shot this bird?"

"Why?" Brad asked in response.

"You know why," the tender boat replied.

A banded eider! On top of that, I took a why-not shot the next day at 50-plus yards, having grown sick of watching longtails skim by way too far out, and be danged if two huge trophy drakes didn't drop hammer dead. Better lucky than good—here's to Hevi-Shot Speed Ball's stopping power. Better still, Linda got a banded eider too, the next morning. My banded drake turned out to be some kind of cross-dresser—the bird was reported as a hen where it had been netted and banded up in Quebec, a mix-up comically explained in a letter from French-speaking biologists in broken English. It so happens a

few males are banded with the 99 percent female birds netted each year when down collectors push the birds to the nets.

A merry trip overall, and we even ate some eider on principle that night, marinated and bacon-wrapped. Surprisingly good, though the huge fresh scallops were not in any danger of going untouched.

As for the new recoil-reduction Flex 500s? Let's just say there's a reason Mossberg has sold over 10 million of these pumps. Recoil was not bad at all, no doubt helped by deep layers of clothes, and malfunctions were non-existent.

THE EIDER GUY

Lucking into a banded trophy drake eider is special, and you can expect your friends to be impressed. Brad Allen, on the other hand, has banded 12,000. Quite an achievement, considering they were down to just a few mating pairs at one point due to overhunting for the valuable down. Allen was not even a teenager when he snapped over birds, long before becoming Bird Group Leader for Maine Department of Wildlife. His father died when he was three, so he's a do-it-yourself guy.

"I got hooked on waterfowl as a kid watching them fly and stage, and decided to be a biologist at 12, when I saw a brochure that said "so you wanna be a wildlife biologist,'" he said. "Those of us that live on the coast have saltwater in our blood. It just gets in your system. I just like hunting sea ducks and teaching guys about it. My only fear is that guys get off a plane and run to the coast and *bang-bang-bang* kill birds and get back on the plane without even appreciating sea ducks, or what a recovery it is."

He thinks the common eider is anything but...common. "Their Latin name translates to 'she of the soft body,' *somateria mollissima*,"

he says. "It is sexy and they are a beautiful duck and when they talk to each other they coo when courting with an *'arooo-aroo'* and that is very sexy, too," he quips.

Allen's amazing eider facts: Eiders almost can't fly with their wing load to surface area, defying laws of flight with their heavy body. They often fly only 10 minutes a day, hitting a mussel bar and then just drifting away. Crippled flightless eiders can live for years and even mate. Total population could be 250,000, and hunters kill 30,000 annually. Money from a commercial down harvest in Quebec goes toward nesting habitat. Most eider hunters are from out-of-state.

"So it's good for economy and we like you guys coming and eating our scallops. People don't understand sea ducks. They think it's 60 million buffalo out there and you can just shoot and shoot them, but you can't. They don't deal well with overharvest. They live to 22 years," he says. As for our banded birds?

"Come to Maine in the last week in May to band eiders. It'll be a good trip with the wife and kids," he says.

Legendary Beaver Dam

Nash Buckingham put the first spotlight on this famed duck club, and it's a field of dreams for greenhead hunters to this day

BY JOHN GORDON

THE DEEP SOUTH IS RICH WITH storied duck clubs, but none are more iconic than Beaver Dam in Tunica, Miss. Long fascinated with its history, I could not believe I was finally going to hunt it.

Oxbow lakes aren't always much too look at, and live lives of relative obscurity. Formed when rivers change course and leave a turn landlocked in the shape of the yoke used for attaching oxen to plows, they tend to be rich in wildlife. The Mississippi River is loaded with oxbows on the deltas of eastern Mississippi that people have hunted and fished for generations, lakes that have remained largely unchanged while the people and landscapes around them have not. They all have names the locals know well.

Only one ever gained national attention, all because of the writings of Theophilus Nash Buckingham. He penned the words that transformed a lake of cypress trees and brush called Beaver Dam into a hunting destination dreams are made of.

Nash told the stories that brought fame to the lake, but he wasn't even born when the men that formed Beaver Dam Ducking Club first laid eyes upon it. They were from Memphis, Tenn., businessmen and citizens of the city that has long been thought of as the Delta capitol. The first expedition took place in the winter of 1878 and the party consisted of four men, W.A. Wheatley, M.L. Selden, J.G. Handwerker, and Tom O'Sullivan. They boarded a James Lee Line steamboat and traveled the Mississippi south to the port city of Austin, Miss. Austin was a thriving community, rebuilt from the ashes after burning at the hands of Union forces. Selden owned land there and had made the acquaintance of Dr. Richard Owen whose family held a large portion of Beaver Dam. Ducks were the quarry, and the lake was covered in them.

MAKING HISTORY

In 1877 Memphis was a bustling city of 45,000. But in the spring of 1878 the dreaded words "yellow fever" were first heard down in New Orleans from ships coming out of Cuba. A viral infection spread by female mosquitoes, it can cause severe liver damage and death. In short time, a full-blown crisis had hit Memphis.

That summer 25,000 people fled and 5,000 died. Only the first frost of fall quelled the epidemic. The men of Beaver Dam would play a large role in the long, slow revival of Memphis, but in the winter of 1878 they just wanted to get away and hunt. They would soon set the foundation for part of sporting history.

Dr. Owen sent a man named Knight with a horse and wagon to meet the party in Austin and escort them to Evansville on the northeastern shore of the lake. He greeted them as they left the steamboat and loaded, food tents and gear for the ride to their campsite near his cabin. The group shot ducks for three days, and birds were so plentiful plans were laid for a return trip.

The next year, they came back and hunted a variety of game, including black bear and deer as well as waterfowl. This was wild country then and there was no easy way to get there. The steamboat journey was long and eventful—a gambler was shot in the chest during a card game on the group's last trip. The men wanted to hunt there more but an easier commute would not come until 1882 when the Illinois Central Railroad constructed the Yazoo and Mississippi Valley line stretching from Memphis to Greenville, Miss. Evansville was a stop, so it became much easier to access the lake and surrounding countryside. Now more of their friends could make the trip and forming a club could be seriously considered. A deal was struck on Dec. 2, 1882, when Wheatley and Dr. Owen agreed to a five-year lease and the building of a clubhouse for the grand sum of $184.84 per year. Beaver Dam Ducking Club was born.

WHEATLY'S INFLUENCE

Railroads soon opened much of the Delta, and they called the train from Memphis to Evansville the "Limb Dodger" because of the heavy forest it traveled through. Pre-agricultural Mississippi was a woodland sight to behold. Bard Selden, great nephew of M.L. Selden, still lives in Tunica County in the community of Hollywood, Miss.

"There was a popular saying in those days that a squirrel could travel from one end of Tunica County to the other without ever touching the ground," he said. "Railroads were the way we traveled when I was young; Hollywood was what they called a 'flag stop' then. If you wanted to board the train, you put up the flag."

With the railroad in place and the deal done, 10 men formed the nucleus of the club. William Arthur Wheatley, known to write under the pen name "Guido," was a central figure. Much of

what is known of the club was chronicled by him in the book, "Blood Lines." W.A. brought in a long-time neighbor from Main Street in Memphis named Miles Buckingham who had a 2-year-old son, Nash. W.A.'s influence on young Nash was strong and Nash commented on it in an article published in the "Flushing Whip" magazine in 1956. He wrote, "Mr. W.A. Wheatley, champion of 'Native' Setters in the post Civil War days, lived just three blocks from us. During my childhood and schoolboy days he was, next to my father, my chief mentor afield. I recall Sunday afternoons when we'd run bird dogs well within the city limits of Memphis."

Beaver Dam became legend as more of Nash's work was published in the early 20th century.

Stories of camaraderie amidst flights of ducks taking wing in the morning mist captivated the American sporting audience.

the water with Nash's setter in a small skiff to return with ducks, quail, squirrels, and rabbits. In his later years, Nash spent much of

In his later years, Nash spent a lot of his hunting time in Arkansas and tried to persuade Horace to move there, but he never left his beloved **Beaver Dam**.

People came to know Horace Miller, club caretaker during the heyday, as an expert guide and friend. He and Nash often took to

his hunting time in Arkansas and tried to persuade Horace to move there, but he never left beloved Beaver Dam.

THE RIGHT 90

Time marched on and a hardworking farmer named Rob Boyd saved his money to purchase two sections of land in 1949 that totaled 1,200 acres. On the northwest corner of one section around 90 acres jutted out into a cypress-studded old oxbow lake. Boyd wasn't pleased—nothing grows underwater. But the soil was rich and he prospered and soon had a house on the land and a family. His sons Francis and Mike worked the farm next to the lake called Beaver Dam with a passion for the duck hunting paradise in their own back yard. Mike's boy, Lamar Boyd, became the fourth generation farmer to hunt ducks among the cypress just as club members did long before. Mike thought others should enjoy hunting such an historic destination and booked his first hunts in 1982. Beaver Dam Hunting Services is now in its 31st year.

"Friends from the local area encouraged me to the point that we did it," Mike said. "We don't own but 90 acres or so on the lake, but

it is the right 90 acres. Ducks never fail to come here year after year."

I had the pleasure of hunting Beaver Dam with the Boyds in early January. We went to one of two blinds just a few hundred yards behind Mike's house. The Mississippi Delta is one of my favorite places on earth: The ground bleeds with the history of the Deep South and all of the traditions that began there. Riding through ancient cypress trees you can see Nash and Horace poling along, English setter in the bow, chasing the game of the day.

Approaching the blind, we slid into a dock on the rear of what appeared to be a large group of trees situated in an open hole in the lake. Stepping out from the boat you enter the blind's interior, spacious and rustic, a very appealing place to be while waiting for the sun to rise. Portholes are spaced across the exterior allowing a hunter to only fire at the ducks in front of him. When ducks are working, all you do is step back from the hole and you disappear

from the eyes of wary waterfowl. It is a solid design.

Lamar positioned himself on one end of the blind, Mike on the other with his black Lab Fraidy. I asked him how she got her name. Mike chuckled at the question and said, "She is a pup out of my dog Molly, a litter she had about eight years ago. This one little female pup seemed afraid of everything so my daughter started calling her 'fraidy cat.' Well the name stuck and she became Fraidy. It's funny because a lot of people think her name is Freddy." She worked well for us all morning but sometimes wanted to do her own thing instead of listen to Mike. "Just like her mother," he said with a grin.

The morning wore on and we killed many ducks, a mixture of gadwall, mallards and three wigeon. Early clouds gave way to blue skies and those emerald green heads shined against the cypress trees. I moved down to the other end of the blind where Lamar had been calling ducks to us all morning with practiced ease. I immediately noticed

the shotgun leaned up against the wall of the blind. "It's an A.H. Fox 12-gauge with 32-inch barrels. It just seemed fitting to shoot a Fox out here in Beaver Dam so I got one," he said. Nash is famous for his shotgun "Bo Whoop," a custom Fox double that now resides at Ducks Unlimited headquarters in Memphis. A closer look at the trigger guard showed a gold inlay of "BDDC 1882" as a tribute to the old club.

Quite a few decoys sprawled around the blind, ranging from Canada geese and gadwall to mallards in different configurations with some pintails thrown in as well. Mike told me that all of their decoys were Greenhead Gear, the result of their relationship with Avery, also based in Memphis. "We have been using their equipment for 10 years now and have fooled many a duck with them. It is a mutually beneficial relationship and we enjoy working with a local company, especially since Memphis played such a large role in the history of the lake," he said while scanning the lake.

All too soon, it was time to leave and head back to reality. We had a great morning, not full limits but close; the experience of the hunt itself far outweighs the harvest every time. Quite an experience indeed to shoot among the same haunts as Nash, his father, and the other Beaver Dam members. I went by the old club site down the road from the Boyd home to have a look at what remains. Horace Miller's house still stands among the trees near the eastern shore but the original clubhouse is no more. I stood where it used to be and could hear the laughter of jovial men still hanging in the air, their spirits forever linked to a place named Beaver Dam.

The Kings of Baffin

Trophy redheads and pintails are the crown jewels of the salty south Texas coast. By Joe Genzel

SCOTT ASHTON YELLED down from his perch atop the boat rocketing across the surface of Baffin Bay's wicked morning chop: "We're going about 30 mph, and 11 miles off shore." He was smiling, looking up from a Garmin watch so technologically advanced it would have made Inspector Gadget blush. I on the other hand, had just swallowed another gulp of gulf water and was white-knuckling a black Benelli, which was already starting to rust from the salty bay water. The rough seas bounced both of us—two guys north of 250 pounds—out of our seats like pinballs.

All I kept thinking about was a childhood memory of my mom telling me not to be such a wimp after our entire family nearly drowned when a rented pontoon boat, over-weighted with linebacker-

sized uncles, started to sink like the Titanic on the open water in northern Wisconsin. I'd never seen so many grownups get ready to pitch out of a boat that fast, and it has stuck with me ever since.

But the perilous ride was worth it. Once our fearless Capt. Marcus delivered us to a stretch of Texas coastline, we all threw decoys and drove holes in the sand, sticking in palm fronds for cover from the ducks and sitting in comfy lawn chairs. The hard part (getting there) was over.

Marcus was still walking back from parking the boat when a pair of redheads came in low. The two drakes darted right into the floaters, showing their white bellies. It should have been a double but

I whiffed on the lead bird. His buddy, I smashed. "It's probably banded," I joked to Scott. And to my amazement, when Jett, our enthusiastic young black Lab, brought the bird to hand, there it was: a little piece of Baffin Bay bling hanging around the diver's ankle. What a lucky/random circumstance.

Scott and I shot a few more reds, pintails and two wigeon, one a gorgeous bird meant for the wall, to complete the Baffin Bay trifecta. Jett made two mega-retrieves on sailed birds, one of which was several hundred yards. The little pup looked like a small black dot by the time he reached the cripple.

It was a truly glorious morning, particularly for me since it took over 24 hours to get to the lodge

after flight delays in Chicago and a too-long car ride in a micro-mini compact sedan. The trip got a little dicey at about 3:30 a.m. when a

three-pack of zebras or aoudad or something (it was a long day) bolted across the road. If you're not familiar, Texas is loaded with

high-fence exotics, and big-game hunters come here to chase African plains game without crossing an ocean.

Ted Gartner of Garmin hosted the trip and picked a unique spot to showcase an extensive line of e-collars, GPS devices and watches—telling time is the least of their capabilities. Baffin Bay is sparsely fished for trophy speckled trout and redfish in the winter, and even fewer duck hunt the undeveloped shoreline surrounded by the famous King and Kennedy Ranches. Pintails and redheads are the birds du jour, but you can also put wigeon, gadwall, teal, shovelers and mottled ducks on the strap. You can shoot mergansers and bufflehead too, but we passed on the mergs.

There weren't any other hunters around when we were there last year, the week before Christmas. The number of boats on the water could be counted on one hand. And it's all public as long as you stay below the vegetation lines of the two ranches that encompass the Bay. The famous King produced the 1948 Triple Crown winner Assault and 1950 Kentucky Derby winner Middleground. You might recall Ford came out with a King Ranch line of trucks in the early 2000s as well. It continues to be a working ranch (over 800,000 acres), where livestock are raised and crops are farmed. They even make their own blankets and saddles on the King.

Why Baffin is so sparsely hunted and fished in the winter is a mystery. Think of all the public places you hunt and all the standing in line at boat ramps or check stations you have done just to get a blind that won't offer a single shot at a duck. There is none of that here. And the sprigs and reds are thick (come in January if you want to shoot some of the most gorgeous plumed out birds on the continent). Yes, there are lulls in the season like anywhere else, but it's typically pretty darned good hunting. Up to 15 million waterfowl winter here, according to Ducks Unlimited.

It is a dangerous place, though, if ill-prepared. Wind and fog can sock you in quick, and the Bay is too shallow in some spots; it's easy to run aground. Our hosts Capt. Marcus and owners Capts. Sally and Aubrey Black of Baffin Bay Rod and Gun Club told us of watching Baffin newbies run their boats up on hidden sandbars at full speed. One day they were wade fishing for speckled trout and redfish, and some guys were thrown wildly from their boat after crashing in the shallows. One of the men was pretty wrecked up and bleeding badly—a gruesome scene.

On the second morning Steve Smith (another Garminite) and I whacked our limits of redheads and shot a nice drake shoveler that was

on the edge of full plumage; the thick green head was still patchy in spots. It was Kelly, Capt. Sally's old black Lab, that made the retrieve, her 1,000th, a cool milestone to be a part of. Many outfitters' dogs make that in a season, but the Blacks are fishermen first so their Labs don't get the same opportunities. Plus, most days you're shooting two pins and two reds, and then it's over, maybe a wigeon or mottled duck too.

After shooting a few birds we ate delicious sandwiches on jalapeno bread and broke out the fishing poles in hopes of a few speckled trout. My fishing experience is limited to farm ponds, old strip mine lakes and those summer vacations to Wisconsin I mentioned earlier. These folks in Texas geek out over

sea trout. There's actually a debate as to who holds the state record for the biggest one. A good speckled trout is 25-plus inches and called a "gator." The official state record is just over 13 pounds. One 15-incher caught itself on the end of my line that afternoon. I guess if you lay into a big one "it's like catching a dining room table," according to Sally, but none of us had much luck.

While Steve and I smacked limits of ducks, Scott and Chris Jennings of DU spent that morning trying to wade through a mud hole after their first stop for ducks was a bust. It was so sludgy, Aubrey had to circle back to pick them both up before Scott, a man who can probably bench press the boats we rode in all week, nearly sunk past his

waders. So when Aubrey told us that was where we would be going in the next morning, all of us had a look of concern. Luckily the lesson had been learned and the bottom wasn't too bad when we jumped out. Just knee deep, and it wasn't far to shore.

With the palm fronds set we all tucked in and waited for the wigeon. Aubrey said this was a killer cottontop hole and we were eager to shoot some mature drakes. But the wigeon never showed; instead it was the pintail show and the four of us killed our two each pretty quickly. All were drakes except an unsuspecting hen that nearly crashed into Steve's gun barrel.

A few mottled ducks buzzed around us, but we couldn't keep the pintails out of the decoys.

Watching so many float by with limits in hand was frustrating, but it's also fun to see birds work with no intention of shooting them. Big flocks of snow geese flew high above us and the sandhill cranes sounded off those high-pitched rattling *cooos*. Oh, how I would have loved to shoot one of those and watch it spastically tumble into the salty bay. Of course crane season didn't start until the following day, and we all had planes to catch.

As far as duck hunting locales go, it's tough to beat the south Texas coast. There are birds everywhere, and good Lord, if you could ever get permission to hunt one of the freshwater tanks on the King Ranch it might be one of the quickest hunts in history—the dabblers love them. Add awesome weather, plenty of open water and not a soul to bother you…who wouldn't want to spend a winter on Baffin Bay?

6 MUST-HUNT Duck DESTINATIONS

Record breeding numbers mean it's time
to stop procrastinating and go on the trip
of a lifetime

BY GARY KRAMER

IN THE PRE-DAWN DARKNESS
WE stowed our gear and loaded the
dog, then settled in for the boat ride.
Our guide Jody pointed the bow toward the dark woods and said "hold
on." Fifteen minutes later we arrived
at a brush-covered wooden blind deep
in the timber. Jody and I sat in the hide
while the two others stood in the water

concealing themselves next to the trunk
of an oak tree. Soon darkness gave way
to dim light and I could see 50 decoys
floating nearby.

The first mallards circled twice before
comeback calls brought the pair within
range. When Jody called the shot, I
looked up to see a flash of wings, fired
and dropped the drake. We let the hen

land—she sat motionless for a few seconds before making a hasty exit. Soon
a flock appeared high above the trees
and we started calling, intense at first
then winding down to more seductive
feeding chuckles and quacks. They made
another pass, dropped into the trees and
over the blocks, side-slipping like falling
leaves between the gray trunks. Jody
barked "NOW!" and we fired. When
the shooting was over, three greenheads
were laying in the decoys.

That was the beginning of a hunt
near Stuttgart, one of six must-see duck
destinations every waterfowler should

1

experience. After logging countless air miles and even more on the road over the past 30 years, here are my top picks:

DESTINATION: Texas Gulf Coast
SPECIES: Redheads and Pintails

One of the most critical wintering areas in the Central Flyway, DU biologists estimate 80 percent of the North American red-heads spend winter in the Laguna Madre, along with pintails and other puddle ducks, too. Matagorda, San Antonio and Baffin Bays are also vast shallow saltwater estuaries protected from the Gulf by barrier islands, and excellent spots for shooting limits of reds and pins.

The 2014 breeding population of redheads is estimated at over 1.2 million, 85 percent above the long-term average. By early October, the first birds arrive with a peak from late November to March. The reason for this concentration? Food. More than 90 percent of their winter diet is shoal grass, an aquatic plant abundant in the protected bays along the Texas Coast.

Pintails show early as well, from as far away as Alaska, to spend the winter feeding and roosting on the backwaters of the lagunas and nearby rice fields. As a result, most decoy spreads include both redhead and pintail blocks. Open water is public in the bays and estuaries and guided hunts abound.

2

DESTINATION: Stuttgart, Ark.
SPECIES: Mallards

Serious duck hunters yearn for a fall in Stuttgart's flooded timber, home to the World Duck Calling Championship and world-class mallard hunting. This is a place where duck populations reach legendary heights and greenheads attain celebrity status. It seems everything in Stuttgart is connected to the pursuit of ducks —you can stay at the Best Western Duck Inn, eat at the Mallard Restaurant and listen to KWAK radio.

The Grand Prairie surrounds Stuttgart, and is a vital wintering area for the Mississippi Flyway. The reason for this concentration of birds is the variety and quality of the habitat. Flooded hardwoods form the cornerstone of it, and much of the green timber flooding occurs seasonally as the waters of the Arkansas, White, Cache and St. Francis Rivers overflow. Many green tree reservoirs are artificially flooded as well. Ducks, particularly mallards, are attracted to these areas to rest and feast on the succulent pin oak acorns.

But timber shoots are not the only type of hunting this region holds. Flooded rice fields offer a mixed bag, especially during late November and early December. You can expect a chance at trophy specklebellys, too.

IF YOU GO: Bayou Meto WMA, agfc.com; White River NWR fws.gov/whiteriver; Five Oaks Duck Lodge, 870-873-4444, www.fiveoaksducklodge.com.

3

DESTINATION: Long Island, N.Y.
SPECIES: Sea Ducks

Since the first waterfowl hunters carved decoys and went to sea in wooden boats, the pursuit of sea ducks has been a sport rich in tradition, practiced by a small but dedicated group. They keep track of the tides and weather, learn the habits and migration patterns of the birds, acquire large decoy spreads, maintain boats and motors and endure cold, wet and sometimes treacherous weather for the singular purpose of pursing tidewater ducks. The allure of the ocean, smell of salt air, feel of a building Nor'easter and uncrowded hunting grounds compel me to seek out coastal waterfowling opportunities.

It's a little-known fact that in the shadow of Manhattan's skyline is some of the best sea duck hunting on the East Coast. Each winter thousands of scoters, long-tailed ducks (oldsquaw) and eiders migrate to the bays and shoal waters of Long Island. For scoters (black, surf and white-winged) and long-tailed ducks it is both a stop over and wintering area; for eiders it's the southern terminus of their fall migration.

Sea ducks are attracted to this region not only for its protected waters but for abundant food supplies. They feed largely on the mussel and clam beds that are scattered throughout Long Island's bays and sounds in water depths ranging from five to 30 feet.

Hunting locales are dependent on the time of year, duck concentrations and ocean conditions. Sometimes its off Montauk Point, the Hampton Bays or in Great Peconic Bay. The hunting is from anchored boat blinds in 30 to 50 feet of water and with a spread of 40 to 60 sea duck blocks. You can go it on your own if you have the proper boat and gear or hire a guide.

IF YOU GO: New York Division of Fish, Wildlife & Marine Resources, dec.ny.gov; Knock 'Em Down Guide Service,knock-em-down.com; Back Bay Outfitter, backbayoutfitter.com.

4

DESTINATION: Alberta
SPECIES: Mallards and Pintails

For first timers, Central Alberta appears little more than a vast expanse of cropland. But a closer look will reveal wetlands, small lakes, rivers, aspen groves and grasslands. This landscape harbors some of the best early-season mallard and pintail hunting in North America.

The vast prairie potholes of southern Alberta are prime waterfowl nesting habitat. Ice-age glaciers scoured the land and left thousands of shallow depressions that seasonally fill the potholes with rain water and snow melt. Often referred to as North America's "duck factory," nearly half the ducks harvested in the U.S. are products of Canada's prairie provinces, with Alberta making an important contribution.

Alongside the potholes are wheat, barley and pea fields. The food provided by waste grain and vast wetlands make the region a major staging area for ducks and geese from northern breeding grounds and a true waterfowl Mecca each fall. Field-feeding mallards and pintails are most abundant, and hunting is in harvested fields where layouts or willow blinds are used for concealment and big spreads draw the ducks in range.

IF YOU GO: Alberta Fish & Wildlife, mywildalberta.com; Black Dog Outfitters, blackdogoutfitters.ca.

5

DESTINATION: Sacramento Valley
California
SPECIES: Pintails, Mixed Bag

From a waterfowler's perspective, California is somewhat of an enigma. With more than 38 million people, it is the most populous state. Known for earthquakes and water shortages, California is also rich in agriculture. It provides critical waterfowl wintering grounds, harboring 60 percent of the Pacific Flyway. Between October and March, more than 4 million waterfowl call California home. An additional 5 to 7 million pass through, and about half the nation's pintails winter here, along with impressive numbers of mallard, gadwall, wigeon, green-winged teal and shovelers.

However, as one might expect, human pressures have impacted the wetlands that support waterfowl. Prior to the Gold Rush of the late 1800s, there were an estimated 4 million acres of wetlands. Today, more than 90 percent of those have been lost to development—agriculture, urban sprawl and industrialization. About 400,000 acres remain, much of it in the Sacramento and San Joaquin Valleys. Here, wetland habitats hang on like drifting ships in a sea of agriculture. These isolated patches are a combination of private duck clubs, Federal National Wildlife Refuges and State Wildlife Areas. Public hunters take note, there are nearly a dozen wildlife areas and refuges in the Sacramento Valley.

IF YOU GO: California Department of Fish & Wildlife, wildlife.ca.gov;
Blosser Outfitters, blosser-outfitters.com

6

DESTINATION: North Dakota
SPECIES: Mallards, Mixed Bag

South Dakota is a tough draw for non-residents , so head north to the other Dakota in late October or early November. If you hit the migration right, expect to see hundreds of plumed-out mallards feasting on harvested fields. NoDak is unique in that private lands are open to the public as long as they're not posted. But it's smart to call the landowner to ask permission just in case deer hunters are using the same fields.

Matt Dahlstrom of Hard Core has been going to NoDak since 2008, and said each year has been better than the next. He actually used to make three trips every season, one for early goose, the next for a mixed bag (greenheads, pintail, gadwall, teal and shovelers) and a late-season hunt for mostly mallards. His group focuses mainly on fields, hopefully finding one with a bit of sheet water if it hasn't frozen over yet.

South central and central North Dakota are optimal destinations as well as Devil's Lake. Your best bet is to find water, grab a plat book and start scouting. But once you find the birds, don't rely on a single field or slough (many fowlers hunt loafing ponds during the day), because there is a fair amount of competition.

"You can find a field with 200 ducks in it and then drive down the road and find one with 800, 900, even 1,000," Dahlstrom said. "Also, if you get permission to hunt, it's possible someone else did too, and they might get to the field before you."

With so many birds feasting in fields, it's preferable to run larger spreads. Dahlstrom will put up to 10-dozen full-body mallards and three- to four-dozen Canada full-bodies with a few spinners. But you can still kill plenty of birds with three-dozen Canada decoys and a Mojo, which was how his group hunted initially.

IF YOU GO: North Dakota Game & Fish, www.gf.nd.gov.

© Matt Dahlstrom

SECTION FIVE
BLAST FROM THE PAST

Stuttgart: Home to King Mallard

BEFORE MAN SET foot on what is now Arkansas, clouds of waterfowl migrated down the Mississippi, stopping along the White River and the bayous that crisscross what is now the Grand Prairie. In 1880, Rev. Adam Buerkle led his flock of German immigrants to a place they named for their hometown, Stuttgart. They cleared the land and planted corn and wheat, all of which were prime duck food. Soon rice was also planted, large reservoirs built, and the ducks had everything they needed in Stuttgart, "The Rice and Duck Capital of the World."

"If it don't have a green head, it ain't a duck," goes the saying on the Prairie. Mallards flock here to stuff themselves with rice, and loaf on the flooded pin oak flats, feasting on plump acorns. Hunting the flooded green timber, locals found mallards readily came to good duck calling, and although the first calls were patented in Illinois, it became a passion in and around Stuttgart. In 1936, the first World's Duck Calling Championship was held on Main Street and won by Thomas E. Walsh of

Greenville, Miss., who mouth-called. Soon wooden calls reigned, made by the likes of D. M. "Chick" Major, Clyde Hancock and Jake Gartner. Still held the first Saturday after Thanksgiving, the prize for the world champ has grown from a $6 hunting coat to thousands of dollars in winnings.

The men depicted in the photo are what you would expect of the Mississippi Flyway—dedicated hunters, shooting either a Winchester Model 12 or 97, Browning Auto-5 or Remington 11. This successful morning hunt included a few Canada geese that plied the flyway until they began stopping short in southern Illinois during the 1930s.

Today, mallards are still king on the Grand Prairie, but weather and drought have sometimes kept huge flocks north. But when the cold fronts snap and water levels rise, Arkansas waterfowling returns to what it once was, with greenheads crashing through the oak limbs.

— John M. Taylor

Whistle-Stop Hot Spot

EMBRACED BY THE Missouri River to the west and the Mississippi on the east, along with numerous interior rivers and lakes, Iowa has been a duck and goose paradise for generations: There's even a town named Mallard. Waterfowl from the Canadian provinces and Dakotas funnel down the big rivers and spread across the state.

Blinds on the Big Muddy resembled floating islands surrounded by decoys. Old timers used wooden blocks from Dodge, Herter's, Mason and local carvers like Bellevue, Iowa's Weykgandt brothers to bring the birds close. Great hunting was also found on the Mississippi's backwater sloughs and islands, where hunters built and rebuilt semi-permanent blinds (spring floods often took them downstream) and watched the mallards pile in.

Getting to a river blind was always a chancy affair due to the huge barges plying the waters. Before the advent of outboard motors and lights, a boat full of hunters could find themselves run down by a barge. The Armistice Day blizzard in November of 1940 was unforgettable. The day started unseasonably warm, but by afternoon it was a raging blizzard, and many hunters perished along the Mississippi.

Market hunting was big business here before being outlawed in 1900. Well-known trap shot Fred "Dood" Gilbert killed 3,000 ducks one year. Scull-boats were popular on the Ol' Miss, many made in Bellevue, by a character named "Catfish" Kaiser. The sculler would put in above a raft of ducks, and using the current and his oar to guide the boat, would float down on the birds. The shooter would rise as the boat reached the flock.

Perhaps the most unique duck hunting took place on the "Duck Special," a three-car train—engine, baggage car and coach—that ran between Des Moines and Spirit Lake. When the train came to a slough full of ducks, such as Gun Barrel Slough between Jolley and Rockwell, it would stop. The hunters spread out, and the engineer blew the whistle flushing the ducks. Conductor William Finnicum said more ducks were killed at that slough over the years than the single locomotive could pull.

— John M. Taylor

Photo courtesy of the Edward J. Moxley Collection

Waterfowling Gold Rush

NORTHERN CALIFORNIA WAS made famous by the gold rush of the mid-1800s. So much so, the city of San Francisco named its NFL team (49ers) after the famed prospectors that flocked to this region, looking to strike it rich. But the ducks that migrate through this part of the state each fall are just as distinguished as the miners who broke rock two centuries ago. From the coastal waters to the fertile inland valleys, California hunters are steeped in waterfowl riches. For thousands of years, ducks and geese have migrated from the Aleutian Islands, Alaska, Russia and western Canada to and through California. Colusa, which lies alongside the Sacramento River is called the Stuttgart of the West, only here you can shoot seven mallards, not four like in Arkansas. Bays like Suisun, Grizzly and Honker to the northeast of San Francisco have been the haunts of waterfowlers for generations.

Duck clubs abounded in the north, frequented by movie stars like Clark Gable, Robert Taylor, Gregory Peck, and other luminaries like Ernest Hemingway. One such establishment has the tumbler from which Gable had his last drink at the club, enshrined in a glass case. Another older club was the Widgeon Duck Club, noted for their rare selection of shotguns.

Apparently, shooting ducks with

smaller gauges was in vogue during the early 20th century. Around 1913, the Widgeon Club special-ordered ten 32-inch-barreled, 20 gauges from the Parker Gun Company. All were DHE-grade, and chambered for 3-inch magnum "Ajax-Heavy" shells. Eight of the guns had solid ribs, two with ventilated ribs, all on No. 1 Parker frames, and one was ordered with an extra set of 28-gauge barrels.

In that era before bag limits, hunters took liberally of the bounty at hand, as the photo of these men in their big touring cars illustrates. The advent of the automobile made hunting in remote areas more accessible, and authors like Nash Buckingham frequently wrote of the convenience of motor cars compared to horse-drawn wagons and buckboards. Still, hunters of this era paddled and rowed heavy boats to the ducks and walked into the tule marshes carrying wooden decoys, gun, shells and some kind of seat so as not completely sink into the soft, watery ground. Some things never change—those tactics are still popular in California.

Although loss of wetlands and water resources are center stage, excellent duck hunting can still be had in northern California. The limits just aren't quite as generous. —John Taylor

Duck clubs abounded, frequented by movie stars like **Clark Gable**... and other luminaries.

Photo courtesy of the Edward J. Moxley Collection

Wide, Wide World of Ducks

IT'S SIMPLY KNOWN as the Claypool picture. Taken in 1956 by George Purvis, a long-time wildlife department information official, it has come to define Arkansas duck hunting.

The image was captured in the middle of a live broadcast of Dave Garroway's "Wide Wide World" on NBC. By the mid-1950s, live television had become widely popular, and Garroway's show was a big part of it.

"My job was to have 300,000 ducks in front of the cameras at exactly 3:14 p.m., on December 23rd," Purvis said.

When you look at the picture and think of Claypool's Reservoir, it's easy to imagine you are looking at the whole thing. In reality, the reservoir covers 1,500 acres and those 300,000 birds occupied only about 40. Putting that many ducks in a confined area at a precise time was no easy task.

There were many hurdles. Purvis had to hide TV cameras, crews, control trucks and the necessary workmen and equipment as well as funnel electricity and telephone lines two miles into the woods. Six telephone circuits were needed to send the audio portion of the program to New York. Camouflaged blinds were built for cameras and operators, one of which was 40 feet up a hickory tree. An additional blind was built for the remote-control truck.

The video went from the camera to the control truck via cable, then to an 80-foot relay tower 1,000 feet back in the woods, then 35 miles to another relay tower, 40 miles to a third tower before being sent to Memphis.

There it was transmitted 1,200 miles to New York, where the audio and video were combined to be broadcast live.

With the electronics in place, the only thing left was to make sure at the pre arranged time there would be over a quarter-million ducks in front of the cameras.

"I had learned by leaving one area undisturbed in the vicinity of the picture blind, then driving ducks with boats on open water and using beaters around the edge of the reservoir, that the ducks concentrated in front of the blind," Purvis said. "I thought we could do it again and at a definite time."

At 3:14 the program director in New York pushed a button and 4 million viewers looked on. Not another duck could be put on screen. To add to the excitement, a rocket holding three blocks of TNT was fired over the ducks and exploded in mid air.

"Then there was another explosion as 300,000 ducks leapt into the air," Purvis said.

While all of that was taking place, Purvis was taking pictures. "Wide Wide World" has since become the answer to trivia questions, remembered by a few who were old enough and fortunate enough to own a television.

The photo, though, has endured the test of time. —Steve Bowman

A rocket holding **three blocks of TNT** was fired over the ducks...

The following articles were previously published in *WILDFOWL Magazine*:

"Finding Your Swing," 2013 Equipment Issue; "Ugly Weather, Beautiful Hunt," March/April/May 2013; "Decoy Dilemmas," September 2013; "Ledges, Labs, and Lobsta!" and "Legendary Beaver Dam, " November 2013; "Duck Calling's Roots" and "Whistle-Stop Hot Spot," Equipment Issue 2014; "Stuttgart: Home to Killing Mallard," March/April/May 2014; "Mexican Revolution," June/July 2014; "For Love of Teal," "6 Must-Hunt Duck Destinations," and Waterfowling Gold Rush," September 2014; "Wide, Wide World of Ducks," October 2014; "The Big Lockup," November 2014; "Season's Just Begun," April/May 2015; "Two Birds Down," June/July 2015; "Kicking the Bluebird Blues," October 2015; "Moving Violations," "Pattern Master," "Sheetwater Secrets," and "The Other Down Under," Equipment Issue 2016; "Prime Time for Ducks," September 2016; "Bills Past Due" and "The Kings of Baffin," November 2016; "Alaska Part I: Cold Bay," "Born to Hunt," and "DIY Duck Ponds," April/May 2017;